HIDDEN

HARVEST

The Rise and Fall of North America's
Biggest Cannabis Grow Op

MARK COAKLEY

ECW Press

Published by ECW Press
2120 Queen Street East, Suite 200, Toronto, Ontario, Canada M4E 1E2
416-694-3348 / info@ecwpress.com

Library and Archives Canada Cataloguing in Publication

Coakley, Mark, author
Hidden harvest : the rise and fall of North America's biggest
cannabis grow op / Mark Coakley, author of Tip & trade.

Issued in print and electronic formats.
ISBN 978-1-77041-085-5 (PBK) | ISBN 978-1-77090-494-1 (PDF) | ISBN 978-1-77090-495-8 (EPUB)

1. Drug traffic—Ontario. 2. Cannabis—Ontario. 3. Marijuana industry—Ontario.
4. Organized crime—Ontario. 5. Drug control — Ontario. I. Title.

HV5840.C32O57 2014   364.1'7709713   C2013-907767-7
C2013-907768-5

Cover design: Tania Craan
Cover images: Burnt joint © cabezonication/iStock;
        Smoking joint © francis black/iStock;
        Plants inside vat: OPP photo.
Type: Rachel Ironstone
Printing: Friesens   1   2   3   4   5
Printed and bound in Canada

The publication of Hidden Harvest has been generously supported by the Canada Council for the Arts which last year invested $157 million to bring the arts to Canadians throughout the country, and by the Ontario Arts Council (OAC), an agency of the Government of Ontario, which last year funded 1,681 individual artists and 1,125 organizations in 216 communities across Ontario for a total of $52.8 million. We also acknowledge the financial support of the Government of Canada through the Canada Book Fund for our publishing activities, and the contribution of the Government of Ontario through the Ontario Book Publishing Tax Credit and the Ontario Media Development Corporation.

Canada Council
for the Arts
Conseil des Arts
du Canada

Canadä

FSC
www.fsc.org
MIX
Paper from
responsible sources
FSC® C016245

ONTARIO ARTS COUNCIL
CONSEIL DES ARTS DE L'ONTARIO
50 YEARS OF ONTARIO GOVERNMENT SUPPORT OF THE ARTS
50 ANS DE SOUTIEN DU GOUVERNEMENT DE L'ONTARIO AUX ARTS

Ontario
Ontario Media Development
Corporation

To Nadia

 # Contents

BOOK I

BOOK II

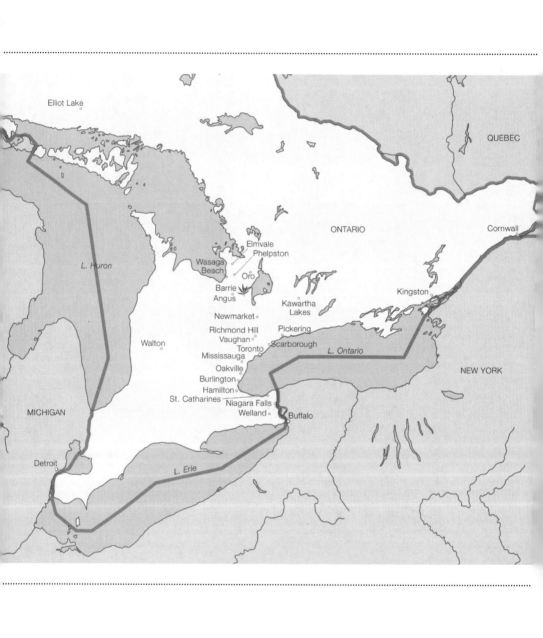

Criminal Organization Hierarchy

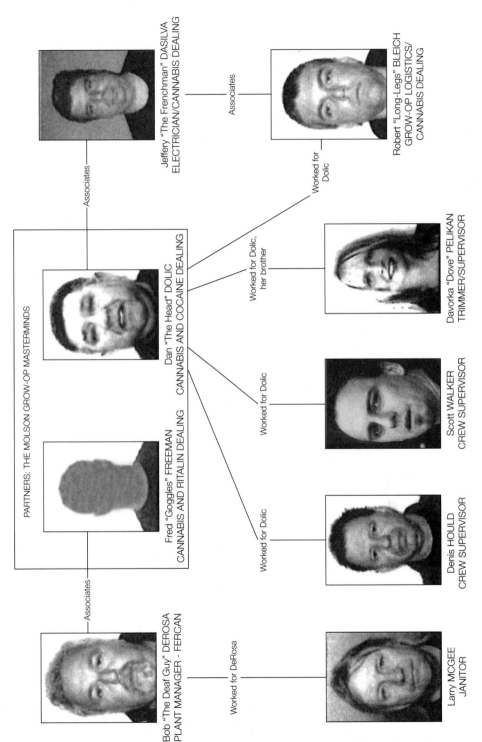

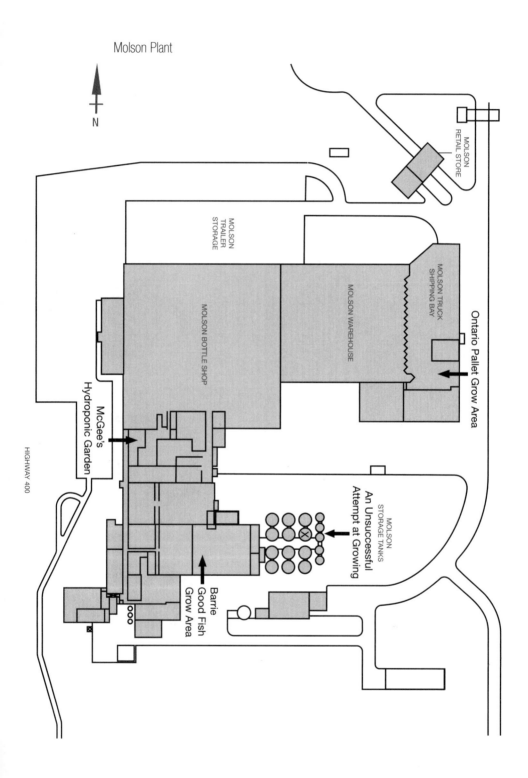

Molson Plant

N

HIGHWAY 400

Ontario Pallet Grow Area

MOLSON RETAIL STORE

MOLSON TRAILER STORAGE

MOLSON TRUCK SHIPPING BAY

MOLSON WAREHOUSE

MOLSON BOTTLE SHOP

McGee's Hydroponic Garden

MOLSON STORAGE TANKS
An Unsuccessful Attempt at Growing

Barrie Good Fish Grow Area

BOOK 1

In an abandoned beer factory in the heart of Ontario, just south of Barrie, there once grew a secret garden. Its legendary flowers, when set aflame and inhaled, would give some users joy; others, relief from pain; others, paranoia; others, dependency; and others, amnesia.

Now that garden is gone.

The jungle of almost 30,000 cannabis plants — with long, finger-like leaves swaying in the humid wind from strong electric fans — thrived under lightning-bright lightbulbs all year long in the giant concrete-walled building by Highway 400. Some of the illegal salad grew in horizontal brewing tanks lined with shiny stainless steel. Some grew in huge rooms, with newly built cinderblock walls covered by sheets of white plastic fastened with red duct tape. And some weed grew hydroponically in a janitor's bedroom.

These hidden harvests of sticky, stinky, all-female flowers would bring to men and women in the illegal conspiracy both highs and lows, fun and misery, wealth and years in prison.

This is the biography of North America's biggest grow op.

. . . .

On flat land at the corner of Highway 400 and Big Bay Point Road, just south of Lake Simcoe's Kempenfelt Bay and the fast-expanding city of Barrie, stood a huge, modernist, gray concrete building. Ranging from two to four stories in height, it covered hundreds of square feet. Around it, a few clumps of road-salt-damaged trees clung to life. There were no other buildings nearby. As large as it was, the Molson beer factory occupied only part of the northwest corner of the vast piece of land. On the exterior wall of the building's second floor, a red-and-white mural reading MOLSON could be easily seen from cars on Highway 400. Barrie is an hour's drive north of Toronto, and the building was a landmark, both to the 150,000 or so local residents and to people with cottages up north. People giving directions would often say, "When you see the Molson plant, you're almost in Barrie."

Enter the Molson Plant [OPP Photo]

The modern history of the property began with tobacco. In 1971, Benson & Hedges — a Canadian corporation owned by U.S. tobacco dealer Philip Morris that made and sold cigarettes in Canada — bought the Barrie-area greenfield for $12 million.

Benson & Hedges put up the building and then took over Ontario's last independent beer brewery, Formosa Springs, which made Club Ale, Diamond Lager, Tonic Stout, Bock Beer, Octoberfest and Birra Italia. The tobacco company moved Formosa Springs to Barrie, expanding production from 80,000 bottles of beer a year to 6 million bottles. Formosa Springs exclusively used Barrie springwater, from a well inside the building — at that time, some of the purest, cleanest water in the world. Only a few years later, in 1974, Benson & Hedges got out of the alcohol market to focus on selling nicotine.

North America's oldest brewing corporation, Molson, bought Formosa Springs and the Barrie property that year, dropping the Formosa Springs label and restructuring the plant to manufacture a number of beers, including Export, Canadian, Canadian Light, Molson Dry, Golden, Molson Light, Excel, Lowenbrau and Durango. About a third of the beer from the Barrie Molson factory was sold across the border to U.S. customers. Most, however, was used in Ontario.

In 1975, 70 acres of unused land south of the brewery was severed and made into an entertainment complex called Molson Park. Its stadium would host big music concerts — Lollapalooza, Another Roadside Attraction, Edgefest, Warped, Live 8 and more.

With various extensions and additions over the years, the Molson building expanded to 440,000 square feet — the size of six soccer fields. By 1996, the plant was producing 567 million bottles of beer (which works out to about 24 million cases, each containing 24 brown bottles and called a "two-four") per year. New labels included Miller Genuine Draft, with its widely advertised "exclusive cold-filtration brewing technology," and Coors Light. A few years later, Molson announced that the factory would close, in order to centralize operations in Carlingview, Ontario. In a protest against the closure, 500 or so Molson workers occupied the factory for a day before departing.

The last bottle of beer rolled off the line in Barrie on August 30, 2000.

The next year, for a price of $8 million, a Toronto-based corporation bought the abandoned beer factory, along with the 36 acres around it, all surrounded by a fence topped with barbed wire.

. . . .

From the outside, the abandoned Molson factory was a near-featureless block of gray concrete. Seen from above, it was shaped a bit like the letter L — or a bent human arm. There were loading docks at the "hand" at the southeast part, where the grain, hops and chemicals used for brewing alcohol had once been taken off trucks. Beer had been brewed at the "forearm," bottled at the "elbow" and boxed at the "upper arm." At the building's north end, the "shoulder," there were more loading docks, where finished Molson product had been loaded onto trucks for delivery to retailers, who then peddled it directly to alcohol users.

The flat, multilevel roof was covered with dozens of white venting tubes, like unlit candles on a birthday cake. Standing on the roof, you had a great view to the north of downtown Barrie and the beach and the bright blue waters of Lake Simcoe's Kempenfelt Bay.

On one side of the building were two brown-painted, cigar-shaped chimneys, each a bit taller than the building. There were also three almost-as-big grain silos — one painted yellow, one orange and one red — attached to the main building by a covered conveyor belt.

To the northeast of the main structure stood a much smaller building that had once been Ontario's only drive-through beer store, with retail staff putting two-fours into the trunks of cars. There were also two separate buildings to the southeast: a storage building and, beside a big water reservoir, a wastewater treatment center.

A big sign went up on the side of the building facing the highway, advertising space for lease.

Inside, the main building was a complex, multilevel labyrinth with lots of exposed, orange-painted girders and tangled masses of green piping. There were orange metal stairs connecting different levels, halls lit by cold, fluorescent ceiling bars, high catwalks of steel grille and a complicated system of conveyor belts.

There were warehouse areas, storage areas, loading docks, executive offices, a tourist beer-tasting suite (known as the Canadiana Room), janitorial closets, machine-operator booths, a yeast room, a hops room, a kegging room, fermentation rooms, aging rooms, bottling rooms, garbage rooms and many other kinds of spaces.

Much of Molson's office equipment, furniture and supplies had been left behind. Charts, maps, contracts, bookkeeping records and other documents related to the old brewery could be found all over the place. Paint flaked from the walls. A woman who later worked in the building would tell police, "The Molson plant was a junkyard. There were toilets, pizza ovens, tiles, sinks — you name it — all over the place."

Throughout the building lurked massive, rusting, dust-covered beer-making machines with analog dials, twisty metal tubes and clunky-looking levers. In the south end of the structure, 120 long, shiny, stainless steel tanks lined the walls.

Once used to make alcohol, the claustrophobic interior of these tanks would later be used to create a safer but illegal drug: a cryptic nursery of forbidden flowers. This highly profitable workplace would employ dozens of men and women, and last two years, earning many, many millions of dollars — a secret, beautiful, doomed garden in the heart of Ontario.

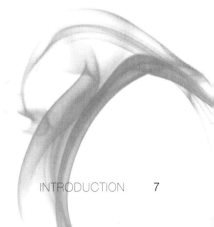

 Mystique

"You want to get hold of your Canadian people now? . . . About this
oil? You got somebody you can call now about this oil?"
— James Kiernan

Summer 1997. Miami.

Glenn Day was a single, 35-year-old Native Canadian construction
worker known to some of his associates as "the Indian." He was of
average height, with a fat belly, and he smoked tobacco cigarettes.
Clean-shaven, he kept his hair short and parted to one side. Other
than hypothyroidism, he was in good health. Day was originally
from a poor family on a reserve near Toronto. He did not pay child
support for his two teenage kids, and he had a record for assaulting a
police officer in 1980, theft in 1981 and mischief in 1982.

A defense lawyer would later describe Day as "intimidating" and
"dangerous." Two of his friends would describe him as being funny
to talk with, a fun guy, a "good bullshitter," a guy who liked to drink
heavily at parties and get "plastered," who gave up alcohol completely
for a while and then went back, who never used illegal drugs, a guy
who smiled a lot — and who was selfish and untrustworthy, in their
later opinion.

Glenn Day, 2012

Now Day carried a fake Florida driver's license and used a fake name, because there was an arrest warrant out for him in that state. The warrant was based on Day's failure to appear at court on a drug charge.

He was a flashy-looking fugitive, with a diamond ring worth $3,500, a $2,000 TAG watch, a diamond earring, $250 sunglasses, expensive suits, a briefcase made of leather and gold, a then-rare cell phone and two expensive BMW sedans. He carried around thousands of U.S. and Canadian dollars in cash.

Glenn Day was in Florida to buy drugs for Drago Dolic, his boss and friend. They had met while both were working in construction in Canada. Dolic and Day shared a home in Richmond Hill, an upscale suburb north of Toronto. They mainly dealt cannabis, and also some cocaine. And they grew cannabis.

Forty years old, originally from Croatia, Dolic had grown up in Ontario, both in the small town of Elliot Lake and the huge metropolis of Mississauga. He was around five-seven and 275 pounds, with bright teeth, and he spoke without an accent. His parents were Muslim. He was in Alcoholics Anonymous. Dolic had a 16-year-old daughter back in Elliot Lake; he had not seen her since she was three and a half.

In the early part of Dolic's farming career, he had constructed a hidden grow op in downtown Toronto: a huge abandoned Molson beer factory at the southwest corner of Bathurst and King streets, just blocks from Lake Ontario. Dolic later boasted about how he had moved discreetly into the rented space in the historic landmark with grow lights and watering tubes and cannabis plants. When the place was to be demolished, Dolic rented another area of the factory, farther away from the wrecking crews. He moved his grow op within the Toronto Molson factory again and again, until the last possible spot was ripped down. Later Dolic would build a much bigger grow op in a different abandoned Molson factory, near Barrie.

In Florida with Day was another friend of Dolic's — Robin Summerhayes, 36, of Oakville, Ontario. He was six feet tall, with long, thinning blond hair. Summerhayes had two Canadian convictions for illegal drugs; for his last conviction — hash trafficking in Brampton, Ontario, in 1984 — he had been sentenced to 90 days in jail. Summerhayes was now married, with three daughters.

Day, Day's girlfriend and Summerhayes stayed at the Sands Hotel in humid Pompano Beach, north of Miami.

For use in smuggling drugs, Day bought a 39-foot Silverton Cabin Cruiser — a sleek, powerful motorboat called *The Casey*, priced at $90,000 — and started taking boating lessons at a local school. But Day was not a great sailor. Once, he crashed the boat into a dock, the home of a restaurant patio; the diners stared at Day after the embarrassing accident. On another occasion, Summerhayes later recalled, Summerhayes spent hours doing maintenance on the boat in the hot sun while Day sat inside his air-conditioned BMW, watching the other man work and not offering to help.

Day hired a local trafficker with a long record, Herbert Johnson, 53 — known as "Skip" — to install fake fuel tanks in *The Casey* for hiding drugs. Johnson had lost his larynx to cancer (caused, he believed, by exposure to Agent Orange as a U.S. soldier in Vietnam) and spoke through a tracheotomy hole in his throat, wearing a voice prosthesis; his speech was sometimes hard to understand. The plan was to get *The Casey* to Jamaica, where Day and Summerhayes would buy drugs to smuggle into North America and sell through Dolic's network.

In addition to Day and Summerhayes, Johnson worked with other traffickers. A police agent in the Port of Palm Beach said he had seen Johnson making modifications to a sailboat called *Mystique*. Because of Johnson's reputation, the police put the boat under surveillance.

Mystique was owned by William Kiernan. He and his brother James, both in their late 30s, had smuggled drugs since they were teenagers. Two years earlier, the college-educated pair smuggled a load of cocaine from the Bahamas to Florida, earning $200,000 in profit. William had used his portion to buy *Mystique*, while James had bought a seaplane (that later sank near Jamaica).

Shortly after the surveillance began, police watched *Mystique* sail out of the Palm Beach marina. On July 21, it was sighted in the Caribbean Sea, sailing south through the islands of the Bahamas. A month later, it was seen passing south between Haiti and Guantánamo, Cuba, toward Jamaica.

In Kingston, Jamaica, the Kiernan brothers met with a man named Keith (known also as "Kappo"), who sold them the drugs. Part of the load consisted of 400 pounds of dried cannabis flowers (known as "bud," the flowers are by far the most psychoactive part of the plant). There were also 280 pounds of cannabis oil onboard. This was made of the plant matter left over after the flowers were removed — the leaves and the stems. (Only the plant's roots were worthless.) There are psychoactive chemicals in the leaves and stems, though in much smaller proportions than in the flowers. To concentrate the drug, the leaves and stems were soaked in a solvent — usually either ethyl alcohol, methyl alcohol, isopropanol alcohol, acetone, petroleum ether or butane. Acetone was a popular choice in Jamaica at this time. (All of these chemicals were dangerous; many people in Jamaica would die or be injured from fires, poisonings and explosions caused by cannabis-oil manufacture.) The solvents pulled chemicals out of the plant tissues, and the solvent/drug mixture would then be strained to remove all solid matter. Putting the liquid residue into a warm place made the solvent evaporate, leaving behind a dark, gooey sludge. This stuff often looked black, but was actually a very dark green, from chlorophyll.

Cannabis flowers contain, at most, 30 percent psychoactive chemicals, while 40 to 90 percent of this sludge consists of psychoactive chemicals.

It takes over 50 pounds of cannabis leaves and stems to make a pound of cannabis oil. The oil is powerful and often harsh on the throat and lungs when smoked. Sometimes it is smeared on a cigarette or a joint. Or it can be dribbled onto a hot coal, smeared on a piece of heated tinfoil or aluminum foil, or squashed between two hot knives, and the vapors inhaled.

Most cannabis oil is not made properly and, as a result, it contains toxic residue left behind from the solvents. These residues can give users headaches or worse. Smoking cannabis oil is often unhealthy.

Mystique was again detected by U.S. authorities as it sailed back north through the Bahamas. When the vessel was 40 miles east of Florida, it was sighted by a coast-guard helicopter, and then intercepted by a coast-guard boat. A team of officers boarded the boat and arrested the brothers, who immediately revealed the drugs, which were hidden in fake fuel tanks. The busted brothers said Johnson had built the hiding place. They agreed to help the police arrest Johnson and the others. The coast guard escorted *Mystique* to a marina in Fort Pierce, Florida.

. . . . . .

On the morning of September 24, 1997, William Kiernan paged Johnson. Johnson, who was in Key West, phoned back. Kiernan wanted to meet as soon as possible, at the Budget Inn Motel in Fort Pierce. Johnson agreed, but first he drove to where Day and Summerhayes were staying in Pompano. He had spoken to them about the cannabis oil and knew they were interested in buying some, if the price was right. Johnson borrowed one of their cars, a

BMW leased to Day's company, and drove to the Budget Inn. He got there around 5:10 p.m.

In room 21, both of the Kiernan brothers wore hidden microphones and tape recorders under their shirts. The police were secretly videotaping the room. The motel air conditioning was noisy, making some of the conversation inaudible, especially when Johnson was talking through his voice prosthesis.

The Kiernan brothers described their voyage, then opened a cooler and showed Johnson a 5.45-pound sample of cannabis and a 1.95-pound sample of cannabis oil. Johnson held on to the samples as they talked. The brothers said they were strapped for cash and needed to get some money fast. James Kiernan mentioned that he had secretly taken money for smuggling expenses out of his wife's savings account and was worried about her reaction when she saw the next bank statement.

James said to Johnson, "You want to get hold of your Canadian people now? . . . About this oil? You got somebody you can call now about this oil?"

"Yeah, I guess," Johnson said.

Bill Kiernan said, "Maybe we can sell part of it. Just get a little bit of cash . . ."

"Well, they said they'd bring 50 grand, 40," Johnson said.

"Fifty thousand?" James said. "To get some of this?"

"Wait, so they got 40 to 50 grand now?" his brother said. "Oh, but they want some of this product?"

"Yes," Johnson said.

"How well do you know these people?" James asked.

Johnson said, "The guy that mixed the oil for Keith [in Jamaica], um, came down and he's known him for 15 years."

The three men discussed Day's offer to pay $1,100 a pound for the oil, a price the Kiernans considered too low. The brothers wanted at least $1,400 a pound.

James told Johnson, "Maybe just sell part of it for $1,100, you know? Maybe they could work on their price a little bit. I mean, you know better than I know. And they're putting a boat [*The Casey*] together right now to run down there, you know? . . . If you want to make a contact and maybe we'll just sell part of this oil to them just to get some cash flow until we can — you know. That way I can get the boat into dry dock and get — at least get the boat taken care of and get . . . everybody some money, and, you know, get everybody some money in their pocket . . . Maybe we should contact the Canadians that own this car [Day's BMW in the parking lot] and go from there . . . Go get a phone card and make the, uh, make the call to the Canadians and see. Just tell them, you know, we're interested in getting rid of some of this. I'll see you in a few minutes then."

Johnson dropped the cannabis and cannabis-oil samples onto the motel bed and went to the door. As he stepped out to use a pay phone to call the Canadians, someone shouted "Police!"

Johnson was arrested and his pager was seized.

The next day, the pager went off a few times, each time displaying the same phone number. When a detective called the number, Summerhayes answered the phone in a hotel room rented under Glenn Day's name. The detective said he was an associate of Johnson's "from the boat" and that Johnson was in the hospital with a medical emergency. The detective said "the stuff" had arrived and some of it was in the BMW Johnson had been driving.

"I'm sitting on the shit," the detective said.

Summerhayes asked for the car. The detective kept talking about how he needed cash, seeming to want a payment. He said he was at the Days Inn in Fort Pierce and gave directions. Summerhayes said he would go there, but first he had to meet with his "other guy" — Day — to get money.

At 2:30 p.m., police watched Day and Summerhayes leave their hotel and put several large bags into a second black BMW leased to Day's Canadian corporation. As Day drove the BMW east along Atlantic Avenue, he abruptly made a left turn into a parking lot, then turned the car quickly around and pulled into westbound traffic. With several erratic driving moves, Day shook off the police surveillance.

But the police knew where the two Canadian men were going and managed to relocate Day's BMW at 6:10 p.m. as it pulled into a McDonalds close to the Days Inn. Day and Summerhayes exited the car and went into the fast-food joint. The police waited. Twenty minutes later, leaving the McDonalds, Day returned to the car and drove away, while Summerhayes walked to the nearby motel parking lot.

Summerhayes went straight toward the other BMW — the one Johnson had borrowed, where the cannabis oil for the Canadians was supposedly stored — and used a spare key to open the car door. He slid behind the wheel and tried to start the engine. But the police had disabled the vehicle. As Summerhayes tried the key in the ignition again, two beer-carrying undercover police agents emerged from a motel-room door and confronted him. They asked him for money for renting the room and guarding the supposedly drug-filled car. Then the men all went into the room, where the undercover officers showed Summerhayes samples of the drugs. Summerhayes handed them $450 and was promptly arrested.

At 10:30 p.m., police at the Sands Hotel in Pompano saw Glenn Day return in his black BMW. Day was arrested, charged, convicted and sentenced to 10 years and one month in a U.S. prison. Summerhayes got the same. Johnson got 11 years and three months. William Kiernan, the owner of *Mystique*, got five years and his brother James got three and a half.

From a Pennsylvania prison — where he complained that his hypothyroidism was not properly treated, causing his fingers and face to turn "puffy and swollen" — Day applied for a transfer to Canada. After a few years in the U.S., he was repatriated to a Canadian prison, where it was more convenient and less expensive for family and friends to visit. Day was banned from ever reentering the U.S.

In the summer of 2002, Glenn Day was released on parole. Drago Dolic drove to Kingston to pick Day up outside the gates of Millhaven maximum security prison. On the road to southern Ontario, Dolic said he would give Day $1,000 a week until Day got back on his feet financially.

Dolic said he had built a big cannabis grow op in the Barrie area, with a lot of guys working for him there, but did not mention the exact location until later. Both men had been involved with many, many grow ops over the years and neither could predict that this special grow op would, much later, turn the two old friends into bitter, irreconcilable enemies, fighting on opposite sides of the War on Drugs.

Briefing

Hops — the leafy vine that grows the bitter-tasting fruit used in beer — is a close biological relative of cannabis. In fact, hops and cannabis are the only two plants belonging to their branch of the natural kingdom.

The Secret Garden

"Hide it completely. Make it disappear. I like things that disappear."
— Jeff DaSilva

Robert Bleich was born in 1974 in Burlington, Ontario. Of Dutch descent, he had dark hair and bright blue eyes. When he was three, his father left, and his mom moved Robert and his baby sister from Burlington to a suburban-style house in a middle-class neighborhood in St. Catharines, Ontario. Soon Bleich and his sister gained a stepfather, of whom Bleich would speak with affection.

"I always had an easy life," Bleich later recalled. "Things were simple growing up. We had some hard times when Dad left. It was tough for Mom. We went on welfare, went to food banks. My mom went to school and studied business and became a medical secretary." Two of his uncles were police officers.

When Bleich was about 15, he first tried smoking cannabis, and soon experimented with two psychedelic drugs — lysergic acid diethylamide (also known as LSD or acid; invented in Switzerland in 1938, this white powder is prized for its ability to create hallucinations) and psilocybin mushrooms (also known as "magic mushrooms" or "shrooms"; used by people since prehistory, these blue-tinged fungi also create hallucinations, gentler than those from acid).

Soon the teen was buying small amounts of illegal drugs from one of his friends and selling it at a higher price to other, less well-connected friends. He later said he started dealing drugs because he "saw friends doing it."

Bleich had gone to public school until Grade 9, but now he dropped out. Fifteen years old, kicked out of the family house by his mom and stepdad, he moved into a friend's place and joined a clique of young criminals who did break-and-enters and used and sold illegal drugs. His various girlfriends didn't mind that he sold drugs. Some of them, who used illegal drugs themselves, appreciated his near-constant supply.

Bleich got half-sleeve tattoos on the biceps and triceps of both his arms: images of castles, dragons, bones and skulls (he would, much later, want to have them removed). He grew up to be tall and handsome. He liked fishing, and went almost every weekend. In the winter, he was into snowmobiling. He was generally polite, friendly and popular, but with a temper that could suddenly explode.

Hanging out and partying with different groups of people was an important part of Bleich's drug-dealing business model. When he was about 17, he started using cocaine. Though he used various illegal drugs for many years, he much preferred alcohol. As a teen, he really liked to get drunk. His favorite brand of beer was Molson.

In addition to earning money through drug-dealing and occasional break-and-enters, Bleich almost always had a legitimate job. He worked in construction and roofing and, for a year and a half, was a full-time chicken-catcher — going into a barn and seizing handfuls of chickens by their thin, scaly legs and stuffing the protesting poultry into boxes going to a slaughter factory.

Twice, Bleich was caught red-handed during a B&E. In 1992, in Thorold, Ontario, he and two buddies chucked a brick through a beer-store window. They got in, pulled a van up to the loading dock and started hauling cases of beer into the van. There were 50 or 60 two-fours in the back of the vehicle when they heard the sound of a siren. Bleich and the other two guys got out of there. Cops were chasing them on foot with tracking dogs and they caught Bleich by some train tracks. He was arrested and convicted.

The next time, in 1994, Bleich was breaking into a deli in St. Catharines with two other guys, prying the back door open and crawling in through the gap. Five minutes later, cop cars were outside, front and back. An officer tried to pull the bent door open to get in, but Bleich kicked the door from the inside, keeping it shut. He and his buddies crawled up into the rafters of the building and scrambled across to an adjoining furniture store where they hid in the dark amid the tables, chairs and sofas. The police eventually found them and arrested them. Another conviction.

Bleich's first and, for a long time, only drug conviction was in 2000 — a possession-for-the-purpose-of-trafficking conviction. He'd been nabbed with an ounce of cannabis, worth $375 at the time; he'd bought it from a friend and was planning to sell it to other friends.

Although he used other illegal drugs, Bleich normally only sold cannabis and cannabis derivatives, such as oil and hash. Sometimes he sold mushrooms and LSD, but never anything stronger, he later said.

Hash is made from the flowers of cannabis plants. These flowers are rubbed, either mechanically or by hand, causing tiny, hair-like glands on the surface of the flowers to fall off. These glands (or trichomes) are transparent stalks with a round bulb at the end, filled with the psychoactive chemicals that cannabis users crave; 90 percent of the drug in a plant is concentrated in the glands, with the remaining 10 percent distributed throughout the rest of the plant (excluding its roots, which contain none). The liquid-filled glands are collected and squashed together into bricks for transport, ranging in color from black to pale yellow. The bricks are cut into smaller pieces for dealing — pounds, half pounds, quarter pounds, ounces and grams. (The illegal-drug world operates with a strange mix of metric and imperial measurements. Most cannabis weight is measured in imperial, except for grams, while cocaine is almost always measured in metric, except for ounces.) Like cannabis oil, hash is often ingested by placing a bit of it on the burning tip (or "heater") of a cigarette and inhaling the combined tobacco/hash smoke, or by squeezing a bit of it between two hot knives and inhaling the rising vapor. (The latter method, whether used for cannabis oil or hash, is dangerous; many unsteady partiers have earned a burn scar on the lips from hot knives.) Hash can be crumbled into tiny pieces and mixed with tobacco or other herbs; this blend can be rolled into a joint or smoked in a pipe, hookah or bong (the latter two are kinds of pipes that filter smoke through water, to make the smoke less irritating and harsh on the throat and lungs).

Bleich made a new friend named Fred Freeman★ (names marked with a star at the first appearance have been changed). Freeman wore glasses, thus the nickname "Goggles." He was a stocky, wide-eyed, dark-haired drug dealer. A bit shorter and older than Bleich, he was originally from Niagara Falls, Ontario. Freeman had never had a legitimate source of income and that would not change for many years. He and Bleich both liked music and partying; they were once photographed backstage at a concert, standing on either side of Ozzy Osbourne. Bleich started buying drugs from Freeman.

When Bleich was nineteen, selling ounces here and there, he also started working as Freeman's "runner." Freeman arranged drug deals over the phone but did not want to run the risk of meeting in person with the other side of the transaction. Bleich would bring an order of Freeman's drugs to a meeting with a buyer somewhere, running the risk himself, and then Bleich would return to Freeman with the money. Some of the money went to Bleich. He was not flashy and tried not to show off his wealth, but could afford things most of his law-abiding peers could not: a car, foreign travel, restaurant meals and booze — plus access to lots of illegal drugs, either free or at wholesale prices.

Before meeting Freeman, Bleich was not involved in illegal gardening. Freeman brought him into that side of the business and helped him learn the basics. Bleich learned about more than gardening, such as the importance of using pay-as-you-go cell phones and tossing them away on a regular basis to disrupt police bugging.

After they'd known each other a few months, Freeman invited Bleich out for dinner. They went to a Chinese restaurant in Richmond Hill. There were other people at the table. Bleich met Drago Dolic, Freeman's boss and the leader of the organized crime group. Dolic was nicknamed "The Head." A self-described alcoholic, he no longer drank but enjoyed watching others drink.

Bleich also met Glenn Day for the first time at the Chinese restaurant. Day was drinking heavily that night. Bleich learned that Day and Freeman had known each other for years and that Freeman and Dolic were partners in several grow ops north of Toronto.

That dinner also marked Bleich's acceptance as a fully trusted member of Dolic's gang. Bleich started hanging out with Dolic, Freeman, Day and, occasionally, Dolic's cute, blond, younger sister, Davorka "Dove" Pelikan. There were some in the gang known only by nicknames, including "Hop Sing," "the Mountie" and "Tripper,"* an occasional police informant.

Bleich was nicknamed "Long-Legs" and Day was called "The Indian." The gang would meet for dinner at nice restaurants two or three times a week — Bleich often ordered lobster, shrimp or caviar, racking up huge bills that Dolic would pay — both to socialize and plan illegal business.

There would also be frequent meetings at "the office," as they called it on the phone, to confuse any snooping police officers. "The office" was a massage parlour in Toronto, near Leslie Street. It was "a legitimate massage parlour run by a Chinese guy . . . not a rub-and-tug," Bleich would later explain. They would enter and put on robes and slippers, then enjoy a hot tub, a sauna, a steam room and a cold dip, followed by time in the lounge, relaxing in La-Z-Boy chairs and watching sports on big-screen TVs. Women would bring them glasses of juice and light their cigarettes. Eventually, a massage would be ordered — either for half an hour (regular), one hour (double-double) or an hour and a half (triple-triple). Bleich enjoyed these meetings very much.

He learned that Dolic and Day lived in the same fancy Richmond Hill house — but were not gay — and that they were partners in a construction corporation. Bleich sensed that they had been friends growing up; later he would guess that they had met in Dolic's hometown of Elliot Lake. Day made a lot of money from his construction work but spent it fast on restaurants, women, booze and his vehicles: BMWs, pickup trucks and a Corvette.

Dolic and Day's house was big and luxurious, in a rich neighbourhood. They had a sauna, a hot tub and a pinball machine. Guys in the drug trade would drop by for dinners, often barbecued steaks. Bleich usually dropped by once a week. People would party and have fun, though rarely loud enough to disturb Dolic and Day's upper-class neighbours. Glenn Day would often get very drunk — "sloshed," Bleich later recalled — though he apparently did not use any illegal drugs. Dolic loved mixing drinks for his friends and watching them drink and get drunk; it reminded of him of all the good times he'd had with booze, before giving her up and joining AA. Dolic usually went to bed earlier than anyone else, at 10 or 11 p.m.

Bleich liked Dolic. He thought the older man was kind and generous. Dolic would lend Bleich money or a car without hesitation. "He loved me," Bleich later said.

Dolic also bought an art piece for Bleich. The laminated-plaque photograph was of an old-fashioned balancing scale. On one side of the scale was a pile of shiny yellow coins; on the other, a baby. Dolic told Bleich that the art symbolized that "you are worth your weight in gold." Bleich was touched. The young man deeply respected Dolic and admired his wealth, his lifestyle and his ability to be both "The Head" and one of the guys.

Being a Canadian drug lord wasn't all fun and games, though. One time, Dolic was kidnapped by guys he knew — they had guns and wanted to hold him for ransom. Dolic's captors tied his hands together and drove him around inside a van. When one of the kidnappers dropped his gun, Dolic tried to grab it. Three or four shots went off in the van as the men struggled over the weapon. During the chaos, Dolic jumped out of the van. As he rolled on the ground, the surface mangled his body. But he made it to a hospital and survived, to the happiness of Bleich and others in Dolic's gang who'd worried that he would be murdered.

Bleich sometimes spent time with Glenn Day. "We were not best buddies," Bleich would later say, "but we hung out sometimes . . . He always had a don't-care attitude." Beforehand, Bleich heard a bit about plans for Day to go to Florida for Jamaican cannabis oil. He didn't learn the details until 1997, after Day was arrested in Florida.

. . . .

In late 2001, a 27-year-old Robert Bleich went with Dolic, Freeman and Montreal-based Jeff DaSilva on a road trip to Barrie. Bleich and DaSilva had never met before, as Dolic liked to keep some of his connections to himself. The men drove north on Highway 400 to the Molson property. Bleich — whose favorite brand of beer had long been Molson — had seen the exterior of the old beer factory building many times but had never been inside before that day.

. . . .

DaSilva was about the same age as Bleich, but shorter and fatter. He was a heavy-bodied electrician with impressive criminal connections in Quebec; he later said of his friends, "Half are millionaires and half are in jail." DaSilva did not drink much, preferring to smoke hash joints. Bleich described him as "a kind guy . . . quiet, mellow, smart."

Soon, the two men became close friends.

DaSilva owned several cannabis grow ops in the Montreal area and built grow ops for other people. He also did some outdoor cannabis farming. He had a criminal record for car theft (at age 19, the year his father died), cannabis production (21 days in jail) and, most recently, possession of stolen property. DaSilva was also involved with cocaine, but was never caught at that.

Around the time of DaSilva's cannabis-production charge, his disillusioned wife walked out on him, taking their young son. After their separation, he signed over the ownership of their house to her. DaSilva's brother had a talk with him about his criminal behaviour, and in time, DaSilva's wife forgave him and they reconciled. "If you ever do that again," she warned him, "I'm going to leave you." Their relationship was good after that. He seemed to be finished with drugs; since the separation, she had not seen him take even a puff of a joint.

Shortly before the failed Jamaican cannabis-oil importation, DaSilva had introduced Dolic to Freeman — the start of a relationship that would deepen over the years, until Dolic and Freeman became very close associates, almost equals. Freeman had not invested directly in the oil scheme but was supposed to take some to distribute when it arrived in Canada.

DaSilva avoided Ontario and usually came to the province only for business. For drug-related meetings with Ontarians, DaSilva insisted on a location around halfway between Toronto and Montreal: the Kingston/Belleville region. At one such meeting, Dolic and DaSilva made the first arrangements for building a massive grow op in the old Molson building in Barrie.

Dolic told DaSilva, as he told everybody who did work for him, that if DaSilva was arrested while building the Barrie grow op, Dolic would pay DaSilva's legal fees in exchange for his silence and loyalty when the police started asking questions.

Dolic would later brag, "If my people get caught, they do the time" — as opposed to "ratting [me] out."

. . . .

At the Molson plant, Dolic, Freeman, DaSilva and Bleich met with Larry McGee, a handyman employed by Fercan, the corporation that owned the property and was controlled by a man named Vincent DeRosa. McGee was a skinny, meek-looking, blond-haired, middle-aged janitor with no criminal record. He lived at the building, often driving around the property in a blue, three-wheeled cart full of tools. McGee had — with Vincent's older brother, Bob DeRosa — worked for Fercan at the Eaton Centre in Hamilton, Ontario, dismantling the escalators and taking out restaurant equipment for resale. He had once lived beside a grow op in Thorold, and when it had been raided, he was arrested, but all charges were dropped.

The four men did not meet with anyone else on this visit. McGee showed them around the huge, empty building that still reeked of beer. Most of the inside lights were on — enough illumination to get around. It was an easy place to get lost in, with many tangles of stairways and catwalks. They toured the whole place, exploring the possibilities of setting up a grow op. Jeff DaSilva was an expert on the subject, Bleich realized. They looked for electrical sources and lines and discussed where they might have to build cinderblock walls. They saw that the building had its own freshwater well.

Wandering around, Bleich found a parka with a Molson logo and a six-pack of full, extra-large, limited-edition bottles of beer. Lots more Molson stuff had been left behind: paperwork, pens, furniture, art, tools and machinery — as if Molson's employees had fled a fast-approaching army, with no time to gather up belongings. Bleich grabbed the abandoned jacket and six-pack; he'd take them home as Molson souvenirs.

DaSilva and Dolic decided that the best place for a grow op was near the northeast corner of the complex, in a vast, open space that had once been part of a maintenance area for trucks.

After government inspectors and the fire department had been through on routine inspections, Bleich went back to the Barrie property and moved in, sleeping on a mattress in what had once been a beer executive's office. Telling his girlfriend he was working at a job-site far away from home, Bleich spent many nights inside the building and worked days alongside DaSilva, the contractor in charge of building for the first part of the grow op. Bleich was in charge of the logistics for both the construction and operation of the grow op; he did very little physical labor. (Bleich later said he worked with DaSilva, not for him, and that, during construction, DaSilva was not his boss but his friend.)

DaSilva brought in francophone tradesmen — bricklayers, carpenters, electricians, plumbers, heating and cooling technicians — from Quebec and got to work. Many of these tradesmen smoked cannabis or drank alcohol while working. The number of tradesmen working for DaSilva varied at different stages of the project; there was an average of six of them secretly working at any given time during the nine months it took to set up the first grow op.

The grow-op electricians, who normally got $60 an hour for similar work near Montreal, were paid $120 an hour in Ontario. Later, Dolic would describe DaSilva's electrical work as "good and clean." And in a Newmarket, Ontario, courtroom, an Ontario Provincial Police officer would also praise Jeff DaSilva's skills, saying the wiring at Molson was better than that at most other grow ops.

Bleich ordered a delivery of cinderblock bricks, which arrived at the property in mid-October, 2001; a few days after that, construction began. The first part of the grow op to be built was the 38-foot-tall, 140-foot-long cinderblock wall, supported by metal girders, separating the grow-op area from the rest of the building. DaSilva's men also closed shut almost all of the entrances to the future growing area, putting up smaller cinderblock walls and welding shut metal doors. The new walls were painted gray, to match the existing walls.

DaSilva later said, "Make an extra wall . . . to hide it completely. Make it disappear. I like things that disappear . . . If the cops — if ever the shit would hit the fan — it would take them a while to fucking find it."

Then the grow-op area's exterior windows — which faced east but also offered a view of Barrie and Kempenfelt Bay to the north — were covered with drywall and heavy plastic. The windows were blocked, Bleich later said, "so nobody could see out of them — or see in, obviously. If people saw lights in the building at two in the morning, not good."

Sometimes, DaSilva's tradesmen would go back to Quebec for a weekend. One weekend, as an experiment, Dolic handed DaSilva a couple of kilos of cocaine to sell on commission. DaSilva packed the powder with the suitcases of some of his tradesmen who were returning to Montreal, but when the tradesmen got home, they found that Dolic's cocaine was too expensive for the Quebec market. They returned with it to Ontario and DaSilva handed it back to Dolic.

DaSilva concentrated on construction and Bleich dealt with almost everything else; Bleich became known as "the main guy on-site." He ordered 20 mattresses from Costco, plus a similar number of pillows and blankets for grow-op workers. He bought food at a local grocery and grow-op supplies at a local Home Depot or at the Plant Products horticultural supply store in Brampton — always paying in cash, sometimes up to $5,000 at a time. On November 23, Bleich signed for the delivery of 90 sheets of insulation. He ordered and arranged for the delivery of many other things as well and spent a lot of time waiting.

There was a set of offices at the north end of the building, nestled high above the former Molson truck-maintenance area. These offices had windows, so the Molson managers could observe the loading area from above. Between the offices and the newly built wall, starting from the bottom, DaSilva and his men constructed two floors out of two-by-ten-foot wood beams and plywood sheets, one above the other. The floors had built-in water shields, in case of flooding.

The crew built a three-level work area supported by steel pillars: the first level rested on the loading area's floor; the second was on top of the bottom level; the third was built beside the abandoned

Molson offices overlooking the loading area, blocking their windows and the view down.

Precise measurement was vital, considering the weight of material to be supported. They used lasers to align beams, and attached the wooden frame to the concrete walls with special bolts that expanded at the tip when fired into concrete, making them almost impossible to pull out.

The first two levels were divided in half by interior walls, creating four very large rooms, all of which would be used for growing illegal flowers. The top level would be used for other purposes, including the growing of "moms" (mature female cannabis plants) and "babies" (also known as "clones" or "cuttings.")

DaSilva sprayed the surfaces of the walls in all of these work areas with a foam designed to block odors. The spray foam stank horribly when it was applied and stuck like glue to whatever it touched. The men had to wear respirator masks, disposable white jumpsuits, gloves and rubber boots when working with the stuff. After the foam dried, they hung white plastic sheets on the walls with strips of red duct tape.

DaSilva's electricians from Quebec were responsible for the next stage of construction. Before they could get to work, though, the grow-op area had to be connected to a source of electricity. There was only one electric meter for the entire building. At an industrial location, unlike a private residence, heavy power usage would not be suspicious — and it would be much less than Molson's had been. The electricity used to grow the illegal product would be paid for in full — not stolen, as with many other grow ops.

So they made a hole in the ceiling just over the newly constructed third level. Around midnight, DaSilva and seven of his tradesmen, helped by Bleich and Larry McGee, dragged the end of a 600-volt Tek 90 cable up and through this hole and onto the roof. It was wintertime and cold out there. "Everyone [was] stoned on blow [cocaine]," Bleich recalled, with a laugh. On the roof, they had to drag the heavy wire, as thick as a man's arm, almost to the far side of the building. "Fuck, we dragged it over a thousand feet or something," said Bleich. It was difficult, awkward work. Partway across, a section of the wire fell off the edge of the building and whipped down onto a vehicle parked below, breaking off its side mirror. After pulling the wire back up and dragging it the rest of the way across the roof, "every fucking person was bruised from here to here on both shoulders," Bleich said. It was "a hell of a night . . . it probably took us three hours to get it up there." They pushed an end of the wire down another hole in the roof, into the partially dismantled machine-bottling area, where McGee connected the 600-volt cable to the building's main power supply. To hide and protect it, the wire on the roof was covered with sheet metal.

The end of the wire reaching into the new grow op was fastened to a shut-off box — like a fusebox in a house, with a switch to kill the power. DaSilva's crew strung wires from the power box to the electrical room on the third level. The electrical room contained 302 ballasts, each weighing 50 pounds, fastened to the walls. (These large blocks of metal filled with chemicals reduced the amount of electricity going through a wire; without ballasts, high-voltage current would make the toxic-chemical-filled lighbulbs explode. Because they got very hot, exposure to water could make the ballasts themselves short-circuit and explode.) Sheets of metal covered the electrical room's walls to protect them from the heat of the ballasts, and fans and air-conditioning units cooled the electrical room. From there, lower-voltage wires ran to the various other rooms requiring electricity.

Jeff DaSilva charged Drago Dolic $3,000 for every grow light (or "candle") installed — Dolic initially paid him $900,000 for 300 candles. Later, the Molson factory grow op would expand to 1,100 candles and cost Dolic almost $4 million more in capital investment.

In case of fire, there were two unlocked exits: one was up the emergency stairs to the roof and the other was down through a trapdoor in the floor of one grow room that was used for bringing in supplies. The usual exit was down the emergency stairs and into the area once used for maintenance of the Molson truck fleet, but the doors at the top and bottom of the stairs were almost always locked

— Bleich and his main assistant, Scott Walker, had the keys. "We put smoke detectors everywhere," Bleich recalled. "And fire extinguishers."

For ventilation, four holes were knocked in the roof over the soon-to-be grow op. Intake machines — known as "bells" — were installed over each hole. McGee had helped them find these intake machines on other parts of the roof and disconnect them to move them over the grow op. Bleich said, "The hardest part of setting it up — the inside is easy. It's the sitting on the roof setting up your air conditioning or your fresh air in and cutting holes in the roof and stuff . . . all the wires."

The intake machines pumped cold air from outside to inside, flowing down through metal tubes — which were covered with spray foam to prevent condensation — to ventilation rooms, where the air would, depending on the season, be heated or dehumidified before being vented to each growing room. DaSilva's heating and cooling technicians put in other metal tubes from each room to suck out the stale, hot air. This used air would be mixed with the lemony-fresh vapors from citronella oil and the smoke from a sulfur burner, which produced a reek like rotten eggs; these two strong-smelling chemicals would conceal the smell of growing cannabis as the air flowed up to vents on the roof and was exhaled into the sky.

DaSilva made sure that air vents did not go straight from a grow room to the roof. Without a few bends in the metal tubes to hide the light from the grow room, the vents would blaze up dramatically from the roof of the building like a spotlight, attracting attention.

DaSilva was the only one of the team who did not sleep inside the building during construction; he slept at a nearby hotel. After a while, Bleich grew tired of living inside this decrepit factory, sleeping every night on a Costco mattress in the old Molson office. He later said he and the Quebec tradesmen became irritable and worn-out from the long hours and hard work. They toiled for 10 hours most days, usually ending at 10 p.m., when they would eat a takeout dinner from Swiss Chalet or Harvey's.

Bleich was paid $600 a week during this period. The reason he was willing to work so hard for such long hours for such relatively low pay was, he later explained, the expectation of much bigger paydays when the grow op was up and running.

. . . .

After almost nine months of work, one of the grow rooms on the ground floor was finally ready, fitted out with metal reflective shields hanging from the ceiling, nozzles for watering hoses on the copper pipe above, oscillating fans with big metal blades, Odor X Tractor carbon filter tubes to absorb odor molecules from the outgoing air, thermostats and more. The crew strung up lights, brought in "babies" (young plants) and started growing cannabis in this ground-level room — room 1 — while construction went on in grow room 2, also on the ground level, and in grow rooms 3 and 4, on the second level.

There would later be a special, non-numbered grow room on the third level used for growing moms and babies, but the first moms and babies in the building grew in room 1.

To operate the grow op, Bleich needed help, so Dolic hired three reliable, discreet gardeners. To supervise them day-to-day, Dolic also brought in Scott Walker — a long-faced, blue-eyed, five-foot-eight, goateed, 41-year-old man from Bleich's hometown, St. Catharines. Walker wore $300 sunglasses, got lots of speeding tickets and would later claim to be a manic depressive. He and Bleich had been friends since their teenage years. Bleich described his assistant manager as "a hard worker, a good guy, trustworthy. He liked to fish, we used to go fishing all the time together, have a few beers."

The gardeners would do all the manual work and Walker would be their on-site manager, leaving Bleich to deal with problems and logistics — like picking up the 90 bales of soil needed every couple of months and buying the $20,000 worth of plant food and $6,000 worth of human food required every month. Bleich's knowledge of illegal gardening came directly from other growers. It was based on practical experience, not theories or scientific jargon. "We didn't need books," he later said.

. . . .

The secret garden began with a plastic-covered tray of 96 tiny cuttings, which had been supplied by Fred Freeman. All the plants were genetically identical — "clones" — and all were female. (Male plants are not as rich as the females in psychoactive chemicals, and they are dangerous: if the pollen from a male plant fertilizes the flower of a female, the female will start to make seeds, expending energy and nutrients that would otherwise go towards making psychoactive chemicals. At the Molson grow op, not a single male plant was deliberately grown.)

To start with, the tray of 96 baby female plants was taken to room 1, watered, given fertilizers and illuminated with fluorescent bars that emitted a special, plant-friendly light spectrum. After a few weeks, the lighting would be changed to powerful, 1,000-watt, pineapple-shaped lightbulbs made by Hortilux or Sylvania. They contained chemicals called metal halides and were known as high-intensity discharges, or HIDs. These expensive metal halide HIDs — which could last a year and were designed for lighting up parking lots, stadiums and highways — were used for most of the growing at Molson. Bleich's crew would also try out sodium halide lightbulbs, which gave off an odd, purple-tinged light spectrum, before deciding that the regular HIDs were a better deal.

On the wall outside each grow room hung a clipboard holding paper schedules. Gardeners would fill in the blanks with data about the crop and leave instructions for the next shift.

After a month, each of the plants had grown thick green stems and wide, finger-like green leaves and was large enough to become a mother herself. Each new mom would then have 10 of her branches cut off with tools that were regularly disinfected to stop the spread of bacteria, viruses and fungi. Care would be taken to make sure no air bubbles entered the severed stems, and the cut ends of the branches would be coated with chemical root hormones to induce the growth of roots. Then the clones would be inserted in small starter cubes of rockwool growth medium. (To make rockwool, put rocks into a furnace and heat until they turn into lava; then spin the lava around and puff it up with air. When cooled, rockwool will look and feel like gray cotton candy.)

As the mothers aged, their overall size would stay relatively small because of all of the stem-cutting. Their age would show only in their central stalk — the older the plant, the more this stalk would become thick, gnarly and covered in tree-like bark. When mothers grew old, they would be killed and thrown away, as elderly female cannabis plants would sometimes become hermaphroditic. (Another odd illegal botany fact: with many varieties of cannabis, the sap of an older plant often changes its color from clear to blood-red.)

. . . .

When the last of the construction was completed in spring 2002, DaSilva and his tradesmen moved back to Quebec. DaSilva and Bleich had by now become close friends. They kept in touch and every Christmas season they met at a restaurant, without their families, for dinner together.

Under Bleich's careful eye, the young grow op thrived. With each mother producing ten babies a month and each baby capable of growing into another mother, it was not long before Bleich did not need any more mothers. Subsequent generations of babies would be grown for their flowers.

After three weeks or so, the baby's root system would be established. Then, while the young plants were only a few inches tall, they would be carried out of the mother room on the third floor to one of the four large grow rooms on the first and second levels. Each room contained about 1,500 plants at a time, each having been transferred (very carefully, so as not to harm the delicate white roots) from a cube of rockwool into a black plastic pot full of Pro-Mix soil. The pots were large, leaving lots of surrounding soil for the tangled, pale root mass to expand into.

The plants — now known as "starters" — would be watered by hand every day, from a rubber hose connected to the plastic tubing on the ceiling that led to water barrels outside the room. To determine how much water a plant needed, a gardener would lift a pot: the lighter it was, the less water the soil contained. Water would be poured around the base stem, but not actually on it; keeping the stems dry protected them from the slimy gray mold known as "stem rot."

Molds are fungi, related to mushrooms. Almost everywhere on earth — especially in warm, humid, indoor gardens — uncountable swarms of mold spores constantly float in the air, each hoping to randomly land somewhere warm and moist, where the spore can reproduce and spread. Mold was worst in the spring, when the humidity was the highest, and a mold attack could destroy a large room of plants in a week.

Plants in pots [OPP Photo]

In irrigation rooms separate from the grow rooms, gardeners mixed water from copper piping with fertilizer chemicals (nitrogen, phosphorus and potassium, plus the other necessary nutrients for healthy plant growth — magnesium, zinc, calcium, boron, chlorine, cobalt, copper, iron, manganese, molybdenum, selenium, silicon and sulfur). The chemicals were dumped and blended into the 10 blue plastic water barrels connected to a motorized water pump that supplied each of the four grow rooms. The proportions of the added chemicals would change based on the stage of plant growth. These irrigation rooms were also used for testing and adjusting the pH level (i.e., determining whether the water was acidic, alkaline or neutral; neutral pH was the best). The fertilizers made the water more acidic, so counteracting alkaline chemicals had to be added to keep the irrigation pH level neutral. Fertilizers could also chemically burn the roots of the plants if the concentration became too strong, so careful measuring and monitoring were important.

There were 80 high-intensity discharge bulbs, or candles, per grow room in this initial phase of the grow op. Each of these phallic-shaped, blindingly bright bulbs hung horizontally under a wing-shaped sheet of shiny metal (known as a shade or reflector) that bounced light down at the plants. The reflectors hung on length-adjustable metal chains attached to ceiling hooks.

The bulbs gave off a lot of heat — much more than the lights used for the babies — so DaSilva's men had installed three five-ton water-cooled air-conditioning units and thermostats in each room. The bulbs were controlled by an electronic timer on a 24-hour cycle — every day, the lights would be on for 18 hours and off for six. This pattern of artificial day and artificial night convinced the plants that it was summer, which to a cannabis plant is a time to grow and to prepare for fall, the season of sex.

Vigorously growing in almost ideal conditions, and without the stalk-strengthening stimulation of outdoor weather, the plants could overextend and become too heavy for their central stalks. Overgrown plants might crack in the central stalk and tumble down. To prevent broken stalks, gardeners tied the central stalks to four-foot-long sticks of bamboo.

A constant supply of fresh air was vital to the success of the grow op. When the lights were on, tiny holes on the cannabis leaves breathed in carbon dioxide and breathed out oxygen and water. At "night," the exchange of gases through the tiny holes reversed. The vents to the roof and large stand-up fans in each room kept the air fresh and moving, letting the plants breathe and making life difficult for mold and bugs.

· · · · · · ·

When the first cannabis crop matured and its flowers were being trimmed, Michael DiCicco — who worked for Vincent DeRosa as a security guard for the property and was a minor player in the agricultural conspiracy — noticed a smell of cannabis in the building and even outside. He would later say, "You couldn't miss it . . . Skunkweed is pretty strong-smelling." So DiCicco phoned Dan Dolic and told him about the smell problem. Dolic passed the word to Bleich. Bleich — who with DaSilva had tried to completely seal off the agricultural area from the rest of the building — searched for where the smell was getting out. It took a long time before he found the crack that was leaking air. It was sealed with Great Stuff expansion foam.

After that, Bleich recalled, "there'd still be an odd smell now and then," but never as strong as with that first crop.

· · · · · · ·

When the starter plants were first put into a grow room, their pots would be placed close together. As they grew, each plant would need more and more space, and the pots would be repeatedly moved apart. Ideally, the lights were kept just above the top of the plants. But as the plants grew, the lights had to be raised — if the plant grew too close to a bulb, the intense heat could burn and damage the plant's delicate tissues.

When the starters grew to be 12 to 14 inches tall — which took about 15 days — it was time to end the growth (or vegative) stage and start (or trigger) the flowering stage. This was done by keeping the lights on for 12 hours and off for 12 hours each day, convincing the plants that it was fall — the time when a male cannabis plant spreads his pollen in the wind and a female cannabis plant captures this DNA-filled pollen for seeds. The approximately 1,500 female plants in a grow room would all continue to grow new leaves and stems, plus a new development — tiny green flowers poking out of their stems. It took about 60 days for the flowers to fully bloom. The light/dark cycle was crucial during that entire time. Any lighting irregularities could turn a female plant into a hermaphrodite, its sudden male flowers blasting pollen particles into the room.

Gender-bending plants were not the only danger the Molson gardeners had to face. Bugs were also a menace. One day, Bleich was in a grow room, looking at some plants in the flowering stage, when he noticed a few wispy white webs on the cola, the main cluster of flowers on top. He looked closer: the plant was infested with spider mites, the worst and most common indoor pest. Mites are not insects but arachnids, related to ticks, spiders and scorpions. Adult spider mites are the size of a grain of salt, barely visible. Their egg-shaped, eight-legged bodies are normally transparent when they are young. As adults, they are white, with a pair of dark spots on the back; except in the fall, when many adult mites turn red or orange.

Spider mites feed by sucking sap from plant surfaces. Like vampires, they fear light and usually spend the daytime hiding, emerging only in darkness. They build webs over their colonies, protecting themselves from predators and from being blown away by the wind.

Spider mites are prolific breeders. The female needs to mate only once to produce about a hundred eggs every few days for the rest of her life — she can lead to a population of a million spider mites within a month. They move from one plant to another by crawling, by gently lowering themselves by silk threads or by hitching a ride on a careless gardener's clothes, hands or tools. An infestation of sap-sucking spider mites will slow a plant's growth, causing its leaves to droop and turn pale. A severe mite attack can kill a plant. The mites thrive in hot, dry conditions, so adding more humidity to the air in the grow rooms might slow them, but it also increases the risk of stem mold.

At first, only six plants in the grow op were infected with spider mites. Then the bugs spread to another 15. The gardeners put all the mite-covered plants into a quarantine area, but soon there was no need for a quarantine area, as the mites had spread to every plant in every room.

Determined to exterminate the spider mites, Bleich bought some 400 mg Doktor Doom Total Release Foggers (or "bug bombs"), which filled the sealed rooms with thick, toxic clouds of pyrethrins and piperonyl butoxide for hours. These miticides killed the children and adults but not the eggs, so in a day or two the spider mite insurgency again flared.

After the defeat of Doktor Doom, Bleich ordered a special miticide spray from the U.S.; it was not sold in Canada because it caused cancer. Using a backpack-style handheld sprayer, wearing a white body suit and a gas mask, Bleich walked among the rows of illegal plants, spraying each of them with the illegal pesticide. It was important not to spray pesticides when the lights were on, because the droplets of cool fluid landing on a hot HID could make the bulb blow up, releasing toxic gas and spraying shards of glass everywhere. Bleich inflicted mass casualties but did not win the war. He never would. "I was always battling them," he later said. In varying numbers, the tiny sap vampires would survive until the end of the grow op. They would survive everything except the police.

The spider mites were not the only pest Bleich had to do battle with — the plants were also attacked by aphids. These insects — each about the size of a poppyseed — like to suck sap, weakening and sometimes killing the plant. (Science fact: aphids poop out concentrated sucrose, which often attracts ants to a grow op.) Like spider mites, aphids are prolific breeders — a female can squirt out up to 100 babies a day. These babies are often born pregnant and, without sex, they give birth shortly after their own birth — their own babies being born pregnant as well. Aphids affect plants just as mosquitoes affect people, by transmitting disease. When an aphid sticks the tip of its sucking tube into a plant, it often also injects bacteria, viruses and fungi into the plant's sap stream.

Trying a natural and organic approach to this problem, Bleich bought a box of ladybug beetles from a garden store. He released these dotted, bright-shelled predators into the grow rooms and hoped for an aphid massacre, but it didn't work. Ladybugs are vicious killers but not too smart; when the lights were on, they would fly up to the HID bulbs and burn to death.

Bleich later guessed that the mites and aphids got in when he brought in some clones from another grow op to fill up one of the rooms. "The bugs would usually happen when the buds were almost done," he said. "I'd try to spray long before that because I didn't want to spray the buds; it's not good to smoke chemicals."

The team learned that the best defense against pests was cleanliness. This came naturally to Bleich. He liked to keep his pickup truck meticulously tidy and would later say, "I would never hire anyone who kept their truck dirty." While they could never completely eradicate the pests, cleanliness kept the problem to a minimum.

Despite the failure of the War Against Bugs, Bleich's garden grew well.

In the flowering room, the virginal female flowers grew in clusters, or buds. The flowers were covered with little hair-like, bulb-tipped glands (known as trichomes) filled with a sticky, transparent fluid. It is unclear why the plant uses so much energy and resources to cover its flowers with these tiny glands, so valued for their effect on the human brain. Maybe these chemical-filled glands make the flowers more sticky, and more likely to catch any wind-borne male pollen. Maybe the chemicals repel bugs or fungi. For whatever reason, the absence of male pollen in the environment causes the frustrated female cannabis plant to grow bigger and bigger clusters of flowers — up to a certain point.

Each of the plants in the grow op would grow to about a yard in height, with one mega-cluster or cola (which could be the size and shape of a cucumber) of flowers at the top, two or three smaller ones on the sides and a scattering of tiny clusters elsewhere (these tiny clusters were not as valuable as the larger ones and were often, derisively, called "popcorn" and sometimes thrown away). The buds at the top of the plant, closest to the light, usually had the highest concentration of psychoactive chemicals and grew the biggest.

During the flowering stage, the plants were switched to a new fertilizer blend, one with less nitrogen and more phosphorus and potassium. At a plant's peak of fertility — 60 days after the start of artificial autumn, just as she was about to give up on the dating scene and stop putting so much energy into her flowers — the trichomes on her flowers would start to change from clear to white, signaling that the crop was also at its peak of commercial value. The gardeners would determine the time to harvest — usually seven to eight weeks after triggering — by looking at the flowers with a magnifying glass. What they looked for, Bleich later said, was "the density of the bud . . . You get crystals spreading and it explodes. The glands open up and release" a sticky, crystal-filled goo.

This was the signal for Bleich's gardeners to harvest. Waiting until morning, when the level of psychoactive chemicals in the plants was at its peak, they would chop off each plant's main stalk at the roots, killing her. Bleich said, "You've got to change the dirt . . . every two [harvests] or every third time or something like that . . . It loses nutrients." Roots and thrice-used soil, along with other garbage (e.g., empty chemical containers), were carried in trash bags out of the building, loaded into the back of a U-Haul truck and driven to a dump, either in Barrie, Wasaga Beach or Toronto. The remaining parts of the plants went to the trimming room.

Each grow room would come to harvest four or five times a year, producing around 2.2 pounds of dried flowers per grow light — or about 50 grams of dried flowers per plant. Bleich and his gardeners would sometimes use the leftover "shake" (cannabis leaves and stems) to make cannabis oil for personal use. He later explained how they did it: "Take a bottle. Fill it with shake. Add two ounces of gaseous butane. It freezes. Drain it, cook it down and make it into honey oil." Other times, they felt it was not worth the effort to make oil with so much free weed all around. "The shake [that was not used for oil] would sometimes be burnt," Bleich said. "Someone would bring it home to burn. Or we'd take it to the dump."

The grow op would eventually have over 21,000 growing plants at any given time and would make 900 pounds of processed cannabis a month — or 10,800 pounds a year. Each pound would sell locally for about $2,500 — which worked out to gross revenues of about $30 million a year. Fifty percent of the profits went to Drago Dolic, who had supplied the start-up capital and had the connections for distribution. Twenty-five percent went to Fred Freeman, as a sort of finder's fee for introducing Dolic to Bob DeRosa, who acted as an on-site property manager. The gardeners and trimmers were paid from the remaining 25 percent.

Whatever profit was left after that was split evenly between Bleich and Scott Walker. Bleich usually earned $40,000 to $50,000 per harvest (or about $200,000 a year). He recalled going out for $1,500 dinners at this time, tossing back lobster and shrimp at high-end restaurants.

Although police would later claim that the cannabis had gone to the U.S. in exchange for cocaine, Dolic said it was all sold in Ontario. He also said he "couldn't grow it fast enough" and "could have had a grow twice the size to fill the orders."

Dolic would later describe secret monthly payments of $86,000 in cash in boxes or envelopes paid to Bob DeRosa, in addition to rent for space at the building, paid with corporate checks. Dolic described how Bob DeRosa had agreed to a rental price at the beginning and then, after the grow op was in place, started demanding huge rent increases. One month, DeRosa demanded double the usual rent. So Dolic paid double. DeRosa also demanded extra payments when the electricity bill was higher than expected. (The average cost of power during the grow op was about $50,000 a month.) Eventually, the monthly cash payments reached $180,000. Davorka "Dove" Pelikan — Drago Dolic's sister and the boss of the cannabis trimmers — later complained that the rent increases were "almost like blackmail," and Larry McGee said Bob DeRosa was "greedy" and kept "jacking up the rent." McGee's friend Michael DiCicco testified in Ontario Provincial Court about Bob DeRosa, saying, "He was a barracuda."

Twice, DeRosa complained about a smell of cannabis in the building that nobody else could detect. He had a loud, in-your-face, tough-guy way of talking. His partial deafness also made business communication difficult. DeRosa was so difficult and unreasonable that Dolic started avoiding him, asking Glenn Day to deal with the landlord's annoying and often aggressive demands.

At least once, Bob DeRosa hid a gun at the Barrie grow op. McGee learned of the gun and (Bob believed) told Vincent DeRosa about it. When Bob learned that McGee had apparently told Bob's younger brother about the firearm, he furiously confronted the slightly taller McGee, calling McGee a "rat piece of shit!" Bob said, "Don't let me come and fucking kill you in front of everybody! I'm in a rage! I'm going to come and kill you in front of everybody!"

McGee punched Bob DeRosa in the mouth.

. . . .

There was a fire-department inspection once in the first year of the grow op and twice later. Bob DeRosa, as landlord's representative, and Larry McGee, as on-site handyman, would guide the Barrie fire inspectors around the building, keeping them away from any part of the building with illegal organisms. Said Bleich, "We'd get a heads-up and have to keep the smell down, turn the lights off to cool it, get the smell down."

On another occasion, a team of OPP officers with dogs showed up in the building, investigating an unrelated crime that involved one of the tenant trucking companies. Bleich watched the dogs nervously. Surely they were trained to sniff out drugs. Surely they would start barking, as they were standing just yards away from an industrial-scale grow op. But the dogs focused on whatever task had brought them there. Maybe the illicit smell was covered by the reek of coffee beans from a coffee-roasting business renting space in the building; if any dog did notice the smell of weed, that dog was not a rat and kept its jaws discreetly shut.

The coffee company, National Roasters, was owned by Vincent DeRosa — who had been in the coffee business for many years — and run by his older brother. It sold cans of Prime Coffee to Giant Tiger and other retailers. Bob DeRosa would later describe himself as a hands-on boss, occasionally putting on a hairnet and helping his employees package the pungent coffee. National Roasters operated internationally, sometimes hiring truckers to pick up raw coffee beans from Texas or to deliver cans of ground, roasted coffee beans in Florida.

DaSilva's Quebecois plumbers had installed copper tubing to connect the municipal water supply to each grow room. "We had problems with the city over the water we used," said Bleich. "We fucked with the water meters. The water going out had chemicals [nitrogen and ammonia]. We got contacted by the city . . . They were coming in there and wondered why — uh, the place is empty and how come so much water's coming out of the fucking place? . . . We had water from the air conditioners, water from the fucking . . . plants, all the extras, you know — washrooms . . . showers, laundry . . . it adds up." A city official with the Barrie water department inspected the building, and was told he could not visit one area because it was being used as a fish hatchery. The official would later testify that the grow op had stolen over $800,000 in water and unreported sewage use. After the problems with the water department, the grow op would switch to getting its water from the well in the building's old brewery. And they would stop dumping wastewater into the municipal sewer. Instead, they used an electric demolition hammer with a chisel tip to cut out square sections of the building's concrete foundation, forming drainage basins, where the used water and chemicals would seep out into the soil and groundwater.

. . . .

At the south end of the building were 44 massive, cylindrical, beer-fermentation tanks, arranged on two levels.

A man named Dave Atlantis★ — who owned an indoor fish farm and a vegetable greenhouse in Sudbury, a few hours north of Barrie, and sold fish and vegetables to restaurants — learned that the Molson plant had a springwater well and many large tanks. Atlantis phoned Michael DiCicco, and the two agreed to go into business together, calling their company Barrie Good Fish. Atlantis told his wife he was "excited" about this new business opportunity.

They brought in experts from the University of Guelph to see if the tanks could be used for raising fish by aquaponics. Encouraged by the experts, Atlantis installed pumps on a few of the horizontal tanks and filled them with water. He introduced some baby tilapia fish into the old beer tanks and, full of hope, started feeding them fish food.

Atlantis worked alone in the fermentation area, relying on his partner back in Sudbury to run their fish farm and greenhouse there. During these experiments, Atlantis was a guest of DiCicco, sleeping at the old beer store. Atlantis never met either of the DeRosa brothers — he dealt only with DiCicco, whom he later described as "a cool guy."

If the fish farm was a success, Atlantis hoped to next try to grow vegetables in the old beer tanks: tomatoes, herbs, carrots, lettuce, cucumbers and zucchini — all fertilized with fish poop.

Atlantis and DiCicco had business cards made, featuring a cartoon silhouette of a smiling fish and a catchy slogan:

HOME OF THE 100% ORGANIC ECO-POND
& AQUA LINK SYSTEM

On the cards, DiCicco was described as President and Atlantis as Vice President of Barrie Good Fish. On behalf of the fish farm, DiCicco signed a lease with Fercan, the building's landlord.

For recreation, Atlantis, his wife and his daughter sometimes rollerbladed through the old beer factory. He knew what cannabis smelled like and never detected a whiff — Atlantis did not know about the illegal growing that Bleich, Walker and others were doing at the other side of the building. After a few weeks, the tilapia fish in the beer tanks were still tiny. For some reason, the fish would not thrive in this environment. After a month or two, they started dying. Atlantis, complaining about "contamination," gave up his experiment and moved his fish-farming equipment out of the building. Allthough there would be no more attempts to raise fish there, a big sign reading *BARRIE GOOD FISH* went up on the side of the building and, every month, DiCicco — the president of a front company that had never sold a single fish or earned a single dollar — would sign a Toronto-Dominion Bank check for $17,500 and give it to Bob DeRosa as "rent."

Briefing

To hide their identity, many of the people at the Barrie grow op used first names only. "Nobody had last names up there," Mike DiCicco later said in a Newmarket courtroom.

Some used nicknames.

A partial list of nicknames used by people connected to the Barrie grow op:

"Allstar"
"Bamboo"
"Bear"
"Bellows"
"Big J"
"Bro" and "Head" (Drago Dolic)
"Bro 2" and "Goggles" (Fred Freeman*)
"Bunk"
"Chief" and "Old Guy" (Michael DiCicco)
"Chubbs"
"Daisy"
"Deaf Guy" (Bob DeRosa)
"Dove" (Davorka Pelikan)
"Fluff"
"Frenchman" (Jeff DaSilva)
"Indian" (used for both Glenn Day and Michael DiCicco)
"JR"
"Kid"
"KM"
"Lex" and "Willie" (Larry McGee)
"Long-Legs" (Robert Bleich)
"Maestro"

"Menace"

"Momb"

"Monster"

"Newfie"

"Ogre"

"Porn Star"

"Rainman"

"Ramjet"

"Rev"

"Slick"

"Smurf"

"Sunset"

"Tripper"*

"Preacher"

"Toro"

"Wicked"

"Wiggles"

"Wonderboy"

....

The Funny Farm

"People were going wacko in there, that's why we call it the funny farm . . . Too much time in closed doors, you know, they go woo-woo."
— Jeff DaSilva

It was after his release from Millhaven in 2002 that Glenn Day got to know Dolic's younger sister, Davorka Pelikan. In her late 30s, with three kids, "Dove" had once lived in Hamilton and now lived in Mississauga. Pelikan was not in good health. She used legal Percocet pills, which contained a mix of acetaminophen (a.k.a. Tylenol) and oxycodone, a powerful narcotic made from poppy flowers.

Oxycodone had been successfully (and falsely) marketed by Big Pharma as a safer painkiller than morphine or illegal drugs. Also called "hillbilly heroin," for its disproportionate popularity in rural areas, oxycodone was very addictive, with side effects including nightmares, amnesia, nausea, itching and sweating. Overdoses were common in Canada, many of them fatal.

Nobody in the world has ever died of a cannabis overdose.

. . . .

Day was hanging around one afternoon with Pelikan and some other women when one of the women told Day that their job was trimming weed and that Pelikan was their boss. At several of Dolic's grow ops, Day learned, Pelikan supervised the other trimmers while she herself trimmed — wielding a pair of expensive, resin-smeared scissors to cut the leaves and stems off cannabis flowers.

Years ago, Drago Dolic had sent Pelikan on a trip to British Columbia. There she had been introduced to a guy who took her upstairs in his house and showed her some uprooted cannabis plants hanging from the ceiling. He taught her how to trim cannabis flowers, and Pelikan learned well. When she came back home to Mississauga, her brother proudly said, "I sent you on vacation and you came back a trimmer!"

Dolic used Pelikan in his drug business a lot because, as family, he believed she could be trusted and would make sure nobody stole from him. She trimmed for him in various places, including Niagara Falls and Wasaga Beach. Pelikan did other illegal jobs for Dolic, including repackaging hash and smuggling drug money to Saint Martin, a small island in the east Caribbean. Mainly, though, Pelikan trimmed.

Of the entire cannabis plant, only the clusters of flowers — the buds and the colas — had any commercial value. Teams of scissor-wielding trimmers got rid of the rest. First, the largest of the leaves and stems would be cut off. The trimmers would find and cut away the valuable flowers, dropping the big buds into boxes and throwing aside every other part of the plant.

Trimmers could work only so fast, and backlogs were bad — plants waiting for trimming could turn moldy. The harvests were staggered, so the plants in the various grow rooms would not all flower at the same time. The crops were timed so that some would be ready for harvest every 10 to 20 days. When trimming was needed, Bleich would pick up Davorka and up to 15 of her girls in St. Catharines. But even with a crew of that size working long hours at big tables under fluorescent lights and a smiley-face wall clock, it would still take a week to 10 days to harvest a single room.

At the Molson grow op, Bleich managed Pelikan and her trimmers and was responsible for their food, supplies and payment. All of the trimmers except Pelikan were blindfolded for the ride north to Barrie, to keep the grow op's location secret, and none of the trimmers could bring cell phones.

Security precautions were especially important when the trimmers arrived because their work would greatly increase the cannabis odor from the grow op. When the blindfolds were taken off the trimmers inside the Molson building, Bleich later said, "the girls didn't know where they were." He said that managing the trimmers involved "dealing with a lot of bullshit . . . a big gossip parade."

Bleich, Walker, the gardeners and the trimmers slept in the former Molson offices overlooking the truck maintenance area. The offices — each about 15 feet square, some painted yellow and some blue, all with blond-wood doors — needed little work to be converted into bedrooms: it was just a matter of clearing out the old Molson refuse and putting in some dressers, beds and mattresses. Even when 20 people were living in this part of the grow op at once, most of the offices remained unused — partly because many of the female workers chose to share rooms.

Near the bedroom area, there was a large space used as a common area and dining room. The chair-table combos (hard, round seats attached to a table, like the kind often used in mall food courts) had been scavenged from the old Molson cafeteria. This room was adjacent to a big kitchen behind sliding glass doors, with four fridges, a stove, a Crock-Pot, a coffeemaker and a microwave.

The common room and some of the bedrooms had windows facing east, through which Barrie and Kempenfelt Bay could be seen to the north. Bleich did not want his trimmers to figure out their location by recognizing such landmarks, so he had these windows blocked with sheets of drywall.

DaSilva had also set up combination bathrooms/laundry rooms, with showers and washing machines and dryers, plus full-length mirrors.

There was sexual tension and drama between the mostly female trimmers, brought in whenever a harvest was ready, and the handful of male gardeners, who worked three weeks on, one week off. "There were single guys there sleeping with certain trimmers, in addition to the [gardeners] who had outside relationships," recalled Bleich. "One guy lost his wife over one trimmer. She was a pig . . . It was like a soap opera. A bunch of guys alone, 10 to 15 girls show up. Didn't matter if they were big, fat, whatever . . . There were parties, drinking, smoking joints. Things would happen. There was some jealousy shit going on . . . A trimmer might see a guy going out of the [trimming] room. She'd put her scissors down [to follow him] and boom-boom. Afterward, she goes back to trimming with mussed-up hair. The other trimmers giggle and say, 'Oh! Where did you just come from?' She'd just smile. That sort of thing would happen here and there . . . Three or four of the trimmers were really attractive . . . There was free weed, all you want, from the leftovers . . . At parties, some girls liked cocaine. But parties weren't every night, mainly just before leaving. After working so much, and a lot of them were smoking weed all day, usually you were too tired to party . . . There was a catfight with the trimmers. Crying. One said, 'I quit.' She came back later . . .

"I missed my girlfriend. I had a cell phone. She would call and I'd say, 'Back by eight.' Then I'd call back, say something came up and disappoint her. She put up with a lot of bullshit. It put a lot of grief into our relationship, that's for sure."

Bleich found that, with time, grow-op workers tended to become complacent, which would reduce productivity. "And that's where the cracking the whip comes in," he said, "and [the workers] start mouthing off and that's where the fights start . . . [and some workers] get fired . . . There'd always be some kind of tension, with people spending so much time together. They'd get fed up with each other." After one 21-day shift, Pelikan recalled, she was "pretty fucked up."

She was not the only one so affected — one of Glenn Day's male relatives got a job there as a grower, but having to spend so many weeks in a row in the building was too hard, so he quit. Day later said, "He couldn't deal with it. He had to get out of there, he said."

Jeff DaSilva recalled, "People were going wacko in there, that's why we call it the funny farm . . . Too much time in closed doors, you know, they go woo-woo."

There were also dramas and conflicts — like the fistfight between Bob DeRosa and Larry McGee — among the conspirators outside the grow area. McGee had an assistant, a devoutly religious heroin addict with connections to the Bandidos biker club, whom another worker later described as "stoned all the time." To replace heroin, he took methadone pills. Without telling anyone, McGee's assistant went around the building collecting plastic-coated, copper-core wire, which he took to a furnace and burned, to remove the plastic. The copper was to be sold as scrap, presumably to buy drugs. But a security guard outside saw smoke coming from a chimney and told McGee, who found that the metal-stuffed furnace was red-hot. McGee told DeRosa about the unauthorized recycling and DeRosa fired him.

. . . .

The trimmers sat around a large table — cluttered with tools and ashtrays and cigarette packages and digital scales — on swiveling office chairs, under fluorescent bulbs, surrounded by boxes and bags of flowers and shake.

Handwritten in magic marker on the wall of the trimming room were various rules:

> NO Liquids in Garbage!
> Everybody cleans
> No garbage on tables
> Box is FULL WHEN I Say it's FULL!!
> NO asking for plants at 12 a.m. and then going to bed!!!

There were more handwritten rules, mainly directed at gardeners, on a photocopied piece of paper stuck to the trimming-room wall:

RULES
$50 fine
1 warning
1. clean up room when finished
2. clean up after filling barrels
3. whole room clean up every Thursday
4. leaf gets dumped every 4 hours
5. clone tools get put back when finished
6. if asked to do something DON'T FORGET
7. do not leave drinks in rooms
8. leave pruning bucket outside every room + bamboo bucket
9. ALL tools stay in hallway when finished
10. if you argue or don't listen, $100 fine
11. boss is always right
12. start time 10 a.m. / room time 12:30 a.m.
$50 fine $50

Also on the wall of the trimming room was a payment schedule and two posters: one of a bong and one of an official-looking man raising a hand and saying, *"THE DRUG ZONE."*

There was a stereo system in the trimming room as well, so the trimmers could listen to music while they worked. Police later found CDs by the Beatles, Ozzy Osbourne and Limp Bizkit. Robert Bleich recalled that most of the music played at the grow op was "'60s, '70s stuff — Zeppelin, Floyd, plus Metallica. Classic rock."

But the stereo served another purpose: hidden inside two of its speakers were tiny video cameras, aimed at the trimming table. Feeds from the cameras ran to Scott Walker's bedroom, where he lay in his bed and watched the trimmers on a split-screen monitor. Also hooked to Walker's four-view monitor were two more cameras — one over the door to the stairs leading to the grow op and the other at the top of the stairs, so that he could monitor who came in and out.

Bleich didn't have a video monitor in his room, but he did have a weapon: a walking cane that — hidden in its shaft — contained a sword blade that he could yank out with a twist of the handle. Bleich's blade was long and sharp. He later said he had bought it at a flea market and kept it, not as a weapon, but "just for fun." He said the risk of the grow op being robbed or suffering other forms of violence "crossed my mind, but never bothered me."

When the latest harvest had been processed, Bleich drove the trimmers home. "I'd go rent a U-Haul; the trimmers would go in back so they couldn't see out a window," he explained. "I'd take their phones and blindfold them if there were windows, like in a van. One time I was stopped by police in St. Catharines. I'd just left Dove's, had five [trimmers] in the back, all of them had some money. I had 20 grand on me for supplies. I opened the back for the cops and said, 'I'm just finishing moving, just dropping people off.' They let us go. I headed for Barrie."

Scott Walker, who handled the day-to-day operations of the grow rooms, kept a diary to record his observations and give instructions to the gardeners. Excerpts:

Sun April 7 (Day 25) — 2002
Room too cold, plants look beautiful but small, triggered too early

Thurs April 11
Room looks great, leaving for weekend, watch for new growth, fuck my room up and die mother fucker

Mon Apr 15
Moved plants and lights. Nobody moved plants for at least days. Lazy mother fucker. Last chance. 50% have reverted back not good. Changing back to 12 hours

Tues Apr 16 (Day 34)
Leaching from plants look good except burnt ones. Did Fulvic spray. AC at back of room not working.

Thurs Apr 18 (Day 35)
Plants look good but they look like they are still reverting back to veg. Not good. The NL [Northern Lights] look a little burnt from food.

Sat Apr 20 (Day 37)
Painted wall today so lights were off for most of the day.

Wed Apr 24
Plants are still growing. I think temp is way too low at night . . .

Apr 28, '02
Some plants have yellow leaves. Spider mites are making webs on a few plants.

Mon Apr 20
Harvested.

June 05
Get dirt, 40 bales.

June 07
Garbage run, dump.

Sat Jul 20
Leached last rows did lots of bamboo. When I was gone Wonder didn't do his job. There was no bamboo done at all, not good.

Sun Aug 11
Room watered by Mike.

Fri Aug 16
Mold is spreading because buds were opened up — stupid.
Harvested.

Wed Sept 11
Scott watered room . . . fucked, way too small, was away for five
days, not taken care of properly, went back to 18 hours.

Mon Sept 16
There will not be much weight, plants are too small.

Thurs Sept 26
12 hours, plants look great, over 80% over 12" tall, triggered today.

Wed – Sun Oct 19
Bugs look bad.

Mon Oct 21 – Sun Oct 27, '02
Bugs are bad. Refilled sulphur burner.

Nov 24
Harvested.

. . . .

Davorka Pelikan worked at Molson for almost two years. She loved the excitement, and the money gave her three kids advantages — such as paying for university — that would not otherwise have been possible. She worked long shifts, between 12 and 15 hours a day, starting at 5 or 6 a.m., for up to 21 days straight. Most trimmers worked 10-day shifts, followed by 10 days off. Some worked 18-hour days. It was good money, but sometimes very boring work, snipping away for hour after hour in a weird, sunless and claustrophobic environment. And while the unlimited supply of free cannabis helped to pass the time for some workers, it could also make them lazy and daydreamy.

When Bleich drove Pelikan and the other trimmers home after they'd spent many days inside, their skin would be pale. Dolic started giving some of the trimmers free vacations to Cancún, Mexico, so they could relax and tan.

On August 14, 2003, most of northeastern North America lost electricity in the second-biggest power blackout in history. At the Molson plant, the ceiling lights went out while Pelikan and others were trimming flowers. There was no backup generator; the entire building was black. Some of the trimmers freaked, thinking it was a police raid, and others kept on trimming in the dark.

The more the trimmers would trim, the more they were paid. Each had a box, and when Pelikan confirmed that it held a pound, the trimmer earned $200. A very fast trimmer like Pelikan could do up to 10 pounds a day, earning $2,000. Most trimmers could process two or three pounds a day. As a bonus, they kept an ounce or two of the THC-rich resin that built up on scissors and fingertips. By rolling her fingertips together, a trimmer could create little balls of cannabis resin known as "fingerhash."

Pelikan wrote detailed paper records about the productivity of the trimmers and paid them in cash. She later described how, when her bosses criticized her about the trimming, she would take steps "to get things done and not get in shit." When her bosses yelled at her for being slow, she would yell at her trimmers to "pick it up . . . They thought I was a bitch sometimes."

Pelikan got $500 a week extra for supervising, but unlike the other grow-op managers, did not receive a percentage of the overall profit. When the grow op was going at full capacity, the other managers would earn up to $30,000 a month. The lack of pay equity bothered Pelikan.

Weighing the bud buckets and other management work took Pelikan away from her own trimming, a loss the extra $500 only partially made up for. And being a boss could be a pain — sometimes there would be 35 people — growers and trimmers and construction workers — all at the Barrie grow op at the same time. Some workers at Dolic's grow ops would go through drug withdrawal; some quit; some got too drunk to work; others were criminals who had to be watched.

Dolic was not overly concerned about his employees stealing from him. He had personally recruited most of the workers, with Robert Bleich's help. Dolic made sure everybody was well-fed and well-treated. He would visit the Barrie grow op every couple of weeks, and every Christmas season, he supplied a pork-roast dinner for his Barrie workers. If a worker had an addiction problem, Dolic would pay for rehab. There was no reason for a worker to betray him, he believed. Even if someone did steal, say, 10 pounds, Dolic felt the loss would be tiny compared to the profit.

As it turned out, there was only one incident of someone at the Barrie grow op stealing cannabis. One of the growers was caught right after his attempted crime and privately warned; then all the other workers were told what had happened and that the next would-be thief would be fired. After the warning, the guy became one of the very best growers.

Despite the monotony and unfair division of profits, Pelikan enjoyed her work. There was money and excitement. Some of the trimmers were her friends, and they took turns doing the cooking. Pelikan's room was painted purple, with a leopard-print bedspread. She often saw police officers near the Molson plant and would find it funny that they smelled nothing — and knew nothing of the secret garden with its bright white lights, spinning metal fans and crowds of people earning fast cash behind gray concrete walls.

The only smell complaints regarding the building came from some residential neighbours on the west side of Highway 400, who occasionally complained about the smell of coffee from National Roasters, the coffee company renting space in the building.

. . . .

Bleich said of running his massive indoor grow op, "Sometimes it was boring, just like any other job." Working and living in the grow op for weeks on end, people found different ways to pass the time.

In the common room, which was plastered with Toronto Maple Leafs stickers and contained a Toronto Maple Leafs beer fridge, there was a bench press with vinyl-covered weights, as well as a few dumbbells. Bleich occasionally worked out here, as did a few of the others. Beside the bench press was a hammock.

In a corner of the common room were three sofas in a semicircle around a TV; Bleich had set up satellite TV from Bell Direct. There was also a DVD player and dozens of discs, including *The Sopranos*, *Something About Mary*, *Pirates of the Caribbean*, *Red Corner*, *Malcolm X*, *The Best of Chris Farley* and *S.W.A.T.*

Some of the workers read newspapers and magazines — *The Barrie Examiner*, *Toronto Sun*, *Chill*, *Weed World*, *High Times*, *Maxim*, *Getting Stronger*, *Auto Trader*, *Easy Rider* and various women's periodicals.

Video games on Playstation II, such as *Final Fantasy X* and *Jedi Knight*, or Xbox were popular. Some workers brought along handheld electronic amusements featuring casino games or *Tiger Woods Golf*. Other pastimes included card games, crossword puzzles and lottery tickets.

For more active excitement, there were three carbon-dioxide-powered Zap paintball guns for fierce battles in the labyrinth of hallways, drywall barriers and abandoned offices.

In addition to recreation there was plenty of food: boxes of Laura Secord and Quality Street chocolate, Chinese takeout from the Mandarin or the Dragon, pistachios, cashews, licorice, chocolate bars, chips and more. The kitchen was stocked with spices as well as three cookbooks and dozens of food products. Workers took turns cooking communal dinners — lots of pasta with tomato sauce, lots of Kraft Dinner. Some tried dieting with Weight Watchers products.

For caffeine users, the kitchen had a coffee machine and cans of ground beans from National Roasters. Sometimes cups of coffee from Tim Hortons would be brought in. Some workers smoked cigarettes, Players being the most popular brand. Others, wanting to quit the habit, brought a supply of nicotine patches.

Some liked to drink: beer, whiskey, wine, tequila, Grand Marnier, Kahlua, Captain Morgan rum, Bailey's Irish Cream, Appleton rum and more. Others favored illegal drugs: smoking cannabis in joints or pipes, or cannabis oil in pipes or bongs, inhaling or smoking cocaine, swallowing pills (Percs and/or methadone — a replacement for heroin — and/or methylenedioxamphetamine, also known as MDMA, Molly or ecstacy, invented in Germany in 1913 for weight loss and known to induce feelings of euphoria and affection).

Jeff DaSilva later said, "Too much Percs [at the Molson grow op]. Too much fucking pills . . . Legs [Bleich] was bad into them . . . I couldn't get him up out of the bed fucking with a sledgehammer before three, four o'clock. Just fucking pills man. That's what they do to you, eh . . . Start taking Percs all day long. Percocet [oxycodone mixed with acetaminophen], Percodan [oxycodone mixed with aspirin], all the little shit, you know. Just some walking zombie. It was good at the beginning but it just went downhill from there."

Bleich denied DaSilva's description. "Maybe I had a few Percs here and there," he said, "but I never had a problem waking up. I did them because I had my wisdom teeth pulled."

Scott Walker also took Percocet at Molson — later telling police that they offered relief for his severe back pain.

There was a lot of pornography in the common area, much of it DVDs from an adult store at 5 Sophie Street West in Barrie — titles such as *Rude Girls*, *Wicked Jenna* and *Beautiful Blondes*. Police would later find a lot more porn — DVDs, magazines and pin-up pics — scattered throughout the grow op, mostly in the bedrooms of the gardeners, where the men sometimes also displayed photographs of their kids, wives and/or girlfriends. Some of the porn was hardcore; some, like the Sunshine Girl calendar and Pamela Anderson pin-ups, was mild. All of the porn was designed for straight males, except a single copy of *Playgirl*. A police officer would later find a copy of *Huge Boobs* magazine on a bathroom sink. (There were also pink body-scrub poufs hanging in that bathroom's shower, presumably for the use of female trimmers.)

There was no pornography found in the bedroom that many of the female trimmers (not including Pelikan) shared. Why did these women share a room, when individual rooms were available for all? Maybe for companionship; maybe because they were nervous living in a strange, locked, windowless compound in an unknown location, working with porn-obsessed male gardeners.

When a team of heavily armored, heavily armed OPP Tactics and Rescue Unit members later entered the bedroom of the trimmers, they violently burst into a tidy space with several beds in a semicircle, pink towels hanging from hooks on the walls and a table cluttered with vases of dried flowers, makeup, incense, menstruation products, baby powder, Oil of Olay, Febreze spray, Kenneth Cole perfume, NeoCitran for colds and flu, edible massage oil, Sex Rock candy, candles in holders and bottles of shampoo and conditioner.

The Tactics and Rescue Unit team would also find — duct-taped to the room's door — a ribbon-tied bunch of dried faded pink roses.

Briefing

Indica: a type of cannabis flower, originally from Afghanistan, that makes users feel relaxed, thoughtful and sometimes drowsy, affecting the body more than the mind. It is effective medicinally at combating pain, nausea, insomnia and lack of appetite. When grown in an indoor garden, indica plants have a strong natural resistance to insect attacks.

Sativa: related to but distinct from indica, sativa grows naturally worldwide. It makes users feel energetic, active, easily amused and sometimes paranoid, affecting the mind more than the body. Sativa cannabis is less effective than indica medicinally, but has the benefit of not causing drowsiness. When grown indoors, sativa has a strong natural resistance to fungus attacks.

Both types of cannabis produce — in tiny hair-like glands concentrated on the female flowers — a complex and still-misunderstood blend of four mind-bending aromatic oils: delta-9-tetrahydrocannabinol (the main psychoactive element, also known as THC), cannabidiol, tetrahydrocannabivarin and cannabichromene.

 # Yellow Submarines

"How big it got — it wasn't supposed to be that big."
— Robert Bleich

A year after the start of the Molson grow op, Bleich and Walker had enough free time to build their own grow op, inside an old barn in the city of Kawartha Lakes, Ontario. Glenn Day helped them construct an airtight shell in the barn. When completed, Bleich and Walker sold the grow op to a local businessman named Pierre Homard,★ Bleich keeping a 10 percent ownership share. Neither Bleich nor Walker told Dolic and Freeman about this grow op, but in the summer of 2003, Bleich's bosses found out about his activities on the side. Bleich later said he believed it was Glenn Day who told on him to Dolic and Freeman. Dolic accused Bleich of a "conflict of interest" — because he was not giving all of his loyalty to his work at the Molson grow op — and fired Bleich, who went back to what he described as "selling ounces here and there, doing my own thing." He denied this was a "falling out" with Dolic and Freeman, saying he remained friends with both after the firing and sometimes visited the old Molson factory.

Bleich was replaced as logistics coordinator by Denis Hould, a middle-aged French-Canadian former miner from Sudbury who'd previously worked as one of the few male trimmers hired by Bleich. He had a goatee, graying hair and a large nose. He was, Bleich later said, "in good shape . . . [a] good hard worker. I liked him . . . Spent a lot of time with him." It was Bleich and Walker who had taught Hould how to grow cannabis..

With the success of the initial grow op in the Molson building — hidden in the northeast corner of the complex, leased by a front company called Ontario Pallet — Dolic decided to expand. In the south end of the building, once the brewery's fermentation room, were 44 huge horizontal tanks of stainless steel on two levels. Each resembled a small submarine.

Dave Atlantis had long abandoned his attempt to grow edible tilapia inside these tanks and his fish-farm technology was long gone. The tanks were now empty. Dolic decided to fill them with lights and leafy life.

He hired a man named Bill Olive★ to build a new grow op in the old Molson fermentation area. As with the initial grow op, construction went in phases. The first step involved blocking off the fermentation area — leased by the front company Barrie Good Fish, Mike DiCicco its fake president — with new walls: some brick, some drywall. Any gaps were filled with a special anti-odor foam. The new walls were painted the same color as the surrounding older walls, making them less noticeable. All but two of the entrances to this area of the building were blocked: one door that led to the rest of the inside of the building and one door going directly outside. Both doors had new dead bolts installed.

When the new grow op was walled off, a couple of Dolic's guys — helped by Mike DiCicco — started turning beer vats into weed vats. Each of the 44 identical, cavernous tanks was about 33 yards long and 8 wide, with very high ceilings and shiny interiors. On the ground level, a row of 11 pairs of tanks was laid end to end. There was a similar setup on the second level of the fermentation area, accessed by metal-grille catwalks. There were also open stairs between tank levels, and Dolic's work crew enclosed these with drywall and two-by-fours.

Each tank had a small opening at the front and back, plus a larger round opening at the front, with a hinged door. On each of the doors was a wheel screw, like those in submarines, to seal it shut. The door was about two feet wide — too small for a big man to get through, but DiCicco and the other workers were all relatively small and could wriggle in and out.

The renovation of the tanks went in stages: first two, then two more, and so on. By the end of construction, 12 out of 22 tanks on the lower level would be converted into grow rooms, as would 11 of the upper 22 tanks. The tanks used were the ones farthest away from the neighbouring National Roaster offices; the closer tanks were left empty.

Dolic's men installed flat platforms on the rounded bottoms of each tank — these platforms would support the growing plants. Electrical wires were strung to ballasts — eventually numbering 800 in this part of the grow up — beside each tank. From each ballast, wires ran to the top of a tank, and through a little hole. Inside, the wire split into many smaller wires, reaching down like spiderwebs to the lights. Each tank held twenty 1,000-watt HID lights, dangling under metal shades hanging from the ceiling by metal chains. (Eventually, there would be 600 lights in use in this part of the grow op.) When turned on, the bulbs would reflect from the shiny stainless-steel interior of the old beer vat — a blinding, superbright, yellowish glare.

The tanks were ventilated in the same way as the grow rooms on the other side of the building — with flexible metallic tubes that brought fresh, cold air down from the roof into the front of the tanks, while more flexible metallic tubing fastened to the rear of each tank sent stale, hot air up to the roof and into the Ontario sky. A huge, cube-shaped air-conditioning unit sat between each pair of tanks, connected to them with flexible, round foil tubes that looked like the legs of a robotic spider.

Each tank also had two powerful oscillating fans moving air at each end — the fans had to be taken apart first to fit into the holes — plus an Odor X Tractor carbon filter and a thermostat.

Bill Olive's tradesmen turned one of the tanks, known as vat 22, into a water reservoir. It was connected with plastic tubes to the old well in the building's southwest corner. (By this time, the other grow op had also switched from using municipal water to using water from this well.) Tubes connected vat 22 to a series of white plastic barrels, just like those used in the Ontario Pallet grow op, for mixing water and fertilizers. The barrels were connected to the tanks by green hoses.

After building the Barrie Good Fish grow op and running it for a while, Bill Olive was fired for always being drunk. He was replaced by Denis Hould. From then on, Scott Walker would run the Ontario Pallet grow op on his own and Hould would run the Barrie Good Fish side.

Walker and Hould, both growing on a 75-day harvest cycle, competed to see who could grow the most flowers per candle.

Part of the electrical system [OPP Photo]

Ballasts and vats [OPP Photo]

The following are excerpts from Hould's growing diary, which shows their level of efficiency and some of their horticultural challenges:

> *Friday*
> *start #9 at 2 pm*
> *start #10 at 6 pm*
> *#9 will start automatically but #10 must have relay connected at 6 pm*
>
> *Sunday night*
> *water #2 then #1 from res [water reservoir] #1*
> *when finished add water to res #1 . . .*
> *pH should be around 6.2 so it will rise to 6.4-6.5 . . .*
>
> *Tuesday night — after mother room work — no cuttings yet*
> *seal up hole (on our side) in wall upstairs. Tape and garbage bags*
> *ok. Close both doors upstairs.*
> *take 30 largest 4" to silo and plant in new pots*
> *plant next largest 4" into #3-4 — 24 each*

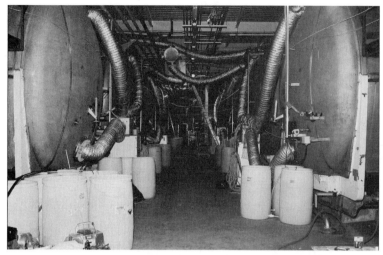

Ventilation and irrigation [OPP Photo]

Wed

add 4000 ml MB [a fertilizer] to Res #2, pH 6.3

mix half hour then pump 3 barrels to Res #1

feed #9-10 from Res 2

feed #3-4 from Res 1 after mixing and adding 6 barrels worth of O_2

what happened to the FILTER SOCKS?

Thurs

spray [pesticide] underneath stock and bottom leaves and any obvious damage

lights off 2 hours before and after spray

¾ backpack each tank

Fri

You keep missing or underwatering individual plants. A half dozen bone dry plants in a wet room means you missed them. Follow a pattern when you water and don't change. Go to the back row of each group of 8 and water each 2 side by side, toward the row. If something looks drier give it double water. Plants that are big get more water than small plants. When it's time to water, all plants should be equally dry regardless of size.

Sat
water 9-10 after midnight
Res #2 — add 2000 ml Humic [fertilizer] ½ hour before starting after watering, refill Res #2 to 10 barrel mark

Sunday
use Res #2 to feed all older and damaged looking trays [of baby clones] . . .

Monday
begin watering mothers at 4:50 . . . cut tops of burning mothers DON'T CUT WOOD IN TANK! . . .

Thurs
. . . When finished, empty out rest of Res #2 on floor, rinse out with big red hose and fill back up with fresh water to bottom lip . . . Wake me up at 7 pm so I can water #5 at 8 pm . . .

Fri
. . . I'M AT DENTIST

On dry-erase boards, Hould wrote out finicky technical rules that highlighted the level of precision and detail needed to make a secret garden thrive:

Watering A Room
1. Make sure hose is hooked to correct Res then check fans and temp in room. Clean out sock filters or room can flood.
2. Move lights to new positions where bud or veging plants are not as big.

3. Raise or lower lights so all are equal distances above the plants. 1' in bud to 3' in veg.

4. Do all necessary bamboo. Bamboo only goes between the side of the pot and the dirt, no deeper than 4". The bud can then lean on the bamboo naturally. Very few tie wraps are required.

5. Water the room. Start at the top of both sides. Do each row of 8 in the same order every time. The wand always goes down the same row. Water the back 2 on the wall first, then the next 2, then lift out the wand to water the 4 on the aisle. While watering each group of 2 plants, it is necessary to look ahead to the next group to decide in advance how much water to put into the pots. Low = 3-4 sec [seconds] = smaller plant — black soil. Medium = 6-7 sec = most of the room. High = 9-12 sec = largest plants — any plant with a soil colour light brown to gray. 5-7 sec = 1¾ liters . . . After plants hit 8", enough water needs to be put in each pot so that water comes out [the bottom of] every pot.

6. Do bamboo again.

7. Check that fans are all pointing in the correct position then take the hose out of the tank.

8. Collect sample of water coming thru sock filter. Check EC and pH and write the numbers in the log.

9. Complete the log, as well as any notes about things noticed.

10. Check Res. Leave running if possible. Make sure bypass is wide open then turn off red valve responsible for the hose. Don't leave hose pressurized.

Later, throughout the Barrie Good Fish grow op, police found checklists, with exhortations to the gardeners to improve their performance in key areas:

Check dry room if it's full. Is exhaust on? Do any trays need work? Temp OK?

*Check what watering has been done. Make sure that water . . .
has food . . . Never use new (chlorinated) water!!!*

Are all the timers working properly?

If candles have been turned on, can they be moved around?

*Check pH meter. Are the readings consistent with readings earlier
in the day? Is there any reason to doubt the meter's accuracy?
Check the meter with buffers every couple of days. Only recalibrate
if really necessary . . .*

Kill many bugs.

There were also sayings, apparently intended to be inspirational,
scrawled on walls:

Anything less than enough is just not enough! Grow more!

I only can please one person a day and today's not your day.

She who wants dick, gets dick.

It's the silence between the notes that makes the music.

. . . .

There would eventually be 21 tanks used as regular grow rooms and
two, with entry holes cut larger for easier access, used for moms and
babies. Each grow tank held 330 thriving plants sprouting in pots of
Pro-Mix and regularly, meticulously hand-watered with a garden hose.

Attached to the outside of each tank, near the entry hole, was a
black chalkboard. Information was regularly written on these boards
— plant-food formulas, shopping lists, instructions and reminders

about the checklists. Attached to clipboards hanging from many of the tanks were blank grow schedules, on which gardeners would write triggering dates, the fertilizer formula used, the pH of the water, the expected date of harvest and so on.

The gardeners and the trimmers slept, ate, partied and relaxed in offices near the tanks. Walker would pick up and drop off the blindfolded trimmers needed on the Ontario Pallet side and Hould would do so for those on his side.

Like the trimmers at Ontario Pallet, most of the female trimmers at Barrie Good Fish chose to share a room. There were photos of naked and flexible women taped up throughout the grow op, including on the sides of the grow tanks. Plus there were Players cigarette butts spilling out of ashtrays, butane cartridges, ratty-looking sofas around a TV, paper plates, red plastic cups, spray bottles of Febreze and Axe Body Spray, cans of National Roasters coffee, boxes of chemicals marked *CORROSIVE* and, almost as prevalent as the porn, items featuring the Toronto Maple Leafs logo.

Near the middle of the tanks was an emergency decontamination shower.

One day, an employee of a salvage company hired to work in the building asked DiCicco about getting into the part of the building leased by Barrie Good Fish. DiCicco said that was not possible — the area was sealed to prevent contamination of the tilapia. "Fish are very susceptible to disease," DiCicco said, "and nobody is allowed back there."

. . . . . .

After being trimmed, the cannabis flowers were taken to the drying room. They would be dumped onto rectangular metal screens with wooden frames and spread out evenly. The screens would be slid into floor-to-ceiling, multilevel wooden racks so tall it took a ladder to reach the top. Every day, each rack had to be taken down, so the buds could be flipped over.

Air conditioners, heaters and dehumidifiers kept the drying-room air at the right temperature and humidity and some oscillating fans kept it moving, which speeded drying and deterred airborne mold spores. As plants dried, spider mites would sense that their meal ticket was ending. They would crawl off the dead plants and set out — against all odds — on epic quests for living sap.

Since more than 80 percent of the weight of a cannabis plant was water, it took a few days for the flowers to dry. Drying them too fast would trap chlorophyll, starch and nitrates in the plant's tissue, making the smoke of the burning plant taste bad. Dried slowly, the plant's water would evaporate evenly and unwanted chemicals would break down, making for a better-tasting, more valuable product.

"When the buds were dried," Bleich explained, "you put them in big garbage bags to sweat them, so the bud dries even. Do it for 24 hours. The moist buds send water to the dry ones. Then put them back on the rack four to five days. They're done when they're crispy on the outside."

The crew would also use a moisture meter: a two-pronged pin they'd jab into the stalk in the middle of a cluster of flowers, measuring humidity as a percentage. "When it hits 13 to 15 percent, give them a final sweat," said Bleich. "Then put them into pound bags — vacuum-sealed bags. The [Gastrovac Pro] machine makes a sucking noise." The sealed bags were crucial, as contact with oxygen caused the psychoactive chemicals in cannabis to break down. Light and heat had the same effect.

After weighing and packaging, Bleich explained, "the pound bags went in duffel bags."

Year after year, the Molson grow op thrived and expanded. Bleich later said, "How big it got — it wasn't supposed to be that big."

Briefing

At least four different and distinct strains of cannabis were grown at the Molson/Barrie grow op: Northern Lights, M39, Purple Haze and Miracle.

Northern Lights is a pure indica, designed to be calming and relaxing. Specially bred for growing indoors, it has big, wide-fingered leaves and, during the 12-hour/12-hour lighting cycle, grows dense clumps of dark green flowers, covered with clear THC-filled crystals and orange hairs. A relatively small cannabis plant, it reaches between four and five feet in height. The dried flowers normally contain 15 to 20 percent THC, almost the highest possible natural concentration. Northern Lights has a sweet smell compared to other kinds of cannabis and an earthy taste. First grown in Holland, it came to North America in the 1970s. It won the Cannabis Cup competition hosted by High Times magazine three years in a row, from 1989 to 1991. Northern Lights is often used in scientific experiments with medicinal cannabis.

M39 is a hybrid of the two main kinds of cannabis plants — it is 90 percent indica and 10 per cent sativa. Indica traits dominate M39; its effect is described as sedate and mellow, although the taste of its smoke is harsh and hash-like. M39 is easy to grow and hard to accidentally kill. It quickly yields denser, bigger flowers than most other strains. M39 was common and cheap in the Greater Toronto Area market at this time, but did not have a good reputation; there were rumors that most of the M39 in Toronto was grown by Asian gangs indifferent to quality, selling M39 low in THC and full of headache-causing chemicals. Because of this rumor, in Toronto M39 was often called "China weed." Much of the M39 grown in Ontario is smuggled to the U.S. M39 is the most common cannabis grown and sold in Quebec.

Purple Haze is a pure sativa. Its effect has been described as energizing, trippy and clean, and it is said to affect the mind more than the body.

Usually grown outdoors, Purple Haze is slender and tall, with deep green leaves, which will, if exposed to low temperatures during the flowering stage, change color to a vivid violet or lavender. The strain is appreciated for its offbeat color as well as its big, dense, resin-sticky flowers. It is said to have been created in Santa Cruz, California, in the early 1970s and named after the Jimi Hendrix song (which, some claim, was named after a type of LSD popular in California in the early 1960s — a story Hendrix always denied, just as he denied all illegal drug use; Hendrix claimed the song was inspired by a dream in which he was underwater in an ocean, surrounded by a purple haze). Purple Haze is said to smell skunky and fruity, and its taste is sweet and sour. Like Northern Lights, its THC level is very high — 15 to 20 percent.

Miracle was grown at Molson, Bleich said, because it has a very faint smell, reducing the risk of someone detecting the grow op. In terms of quality, Bleich said that Miracle "was good . . . with big buds, lots of weight . . . it was a government strain from California."

The Old Man and the Seed

"When he is angry and maybe he has been drinking a bit, he sounds like he's going to kill somebody, but he's not even able to kill a fly when he drinks."
— Bob DeRosa's mom

Michael DiCicco had several health problems, including diabetes (for which he would inject himself with insulin), a weak heart and low testosterone levels; he had a handicapped parking permit and walked with a slight limp. He owned a rifle and a shotgun and liked hunting. Five-foot-six, 59 and of Italian descent, he had brown eyes, puffy cheeks, a big nose and graying hair that he combed back. To many people, DiCicco looked Native, leading to his nicknames of "Chief" and "Indian." Another of his nicknames was "the Old Man."

He had a criminal record dating back to the late 1960s, for possession of stolen property, public mischief, failure to remain at the scene of an accident, drunk driving and theft. He had *"C.H."* — the initials of an ex-girlfriend — tattooed on his upper right arm. And he now had four children: two daughters and two sons (one of his adult sons had recently died). DiCicco was a heavy tobacco smoker — his voice was hoarse.

Through a mutual acquaintance, DiCicco knew Drago Dolic. In 2001, Dolic had phoned DiCicco to offer him a job. After many years of working as a mechanical engineer for Shell Canada and the City of Toronto, as well as working security and managing buildings, DiCicco was unemployed and definitely interested in a job. He learned that Vincent DeRosa's corporation had recently bought the old Molson factory near Barrie and was leasing parts of it to different companies.

DiCicco was hired by Vincent DeRosa's corporation and moved onto the property. His new, rent-free home was just northeast of the main building, in a 3,500-square-foot structure that had once been a drive-through Molson retail outlet; it was referred to as "the old beer store." His jobs included security, as well as maintenance of the automatic boilers that heated the huge building; these old and unreliable boilers required an engineer to be on-site 24 hours a day, feeding various chemicals into the boilers and handling burst pipes and other emergencies.

DiCicco's work as engineer often brought him to the beer-factory building, and for eight or nine hours a night, DiCicco worked at the guardhouse at the main entrance to the property, raising the gate to let in vehicles with business on the premises.

After a week at the job, DiCicco was told by Dolic that a cannabis grow up was being constructed in the northwest end of the building — the "shoulder" — near the loading docks. This 30,000-square-foot area was leased to a company called Ontario Pallet, which supposedly made and sold wooden pallets, or skids. Talking to DaSilva's men from Montreal, DiCicco learned that this grow op was owned and managed by Dolic and his associate from Niagara Falls, Fred Freeman. Freeman had introduced Dolic to Bob DeRosa, the older brother of Vincent, who owned of the property. DiCicco didn't like Bob, who — in addition to managing coffee and water-bottling companies from offices in the building, both companies owned by his younger brother — also acted as a landlord's representative and on-site manager. He would later say that Bob DeRosa "was not the most pleasant person in the world . . . [He wanted] everything for him, nobody else."

But DiCicco had a positive impression of Vincent DeRosa, who visited his property almost every Saturday in his black BMW, staying for an hour or so; Vincent also attended the yearly Christmas party there. He was 40 years old, five-foot-six with a strong build, and was described by one employee as "clean-cut and businesslike," often smoking an expensive cigar. He had light-colored hair and bright blue eyes and a deep, intelligent-sounding voice. At this time, his net worth was $50.8 million and he owned 50 or so properties across Ontario. (He had started his career as a Motorola cell phone distributor before building a real estate empire.)

Bob, on the other hand, was scruffy, 52 years old, had a graying beard and was usually in a grumpy mood. He was three inches taller and much fatter than his younger brother, with dark brown eyes. One employee described Bob DeRosa as a "shaggy-looking fella . . . Didn't look very professional . . . He always looked like he just got out of bed."

Bob had a serious chronic back injury, caused by loading a farm truck many years earlier. Because of the resulting pain, he smoked a lot of cannabis — legally, with his official "Authorization to Possess Dried Marihuana for Medical Purposes" certificate from Health Canada. He was also partially deaf: the hearing loss had happened almost overnight, a few years before. He had learned how to read lips, but did not know sign language. He avoided talking on the phone or returning phone messages; he much preferred texts.

Born in Montreal in 1959, the year after his parents immigrated from the Italian city of Napoli, Bob DeRosa moved with his family 12 years later to a 14-acre fruit farm between St. Catharines and Niagara-on-the-Lake. After high school, he opened an autobody shop in St. Catharines. In 1974, when he was in his mid-20s, Bob bought cocaine from a cartel based in Santa Marta, Colombia, and arranged to smuggle it westward through the Panama Canal, but the ship was searched and the cocaine seized by Panamanian authorities.

When his autobody business failed in the early 1980s, Bob started a chain of four or five jewellery stores in southern Ontario. This lasted until the mid-1990s, when he and his family moved to Cuba, to try to import medical and consumer goods from Canada. He was still involved in cocaine smuggling, dealing with the Colombian Santa Marta cartel for his supply and with some Vietnamese brothers who owned a chain of fish stores for distribution — the cocaine was smuggled into North America hidden inside fish.

Bob DeRosa became fluent in Spanish, in addition to English and Italian, though he still used interpreters when dealing with Colombian cartels, to avoid any misunderstandings. After two years in Cuba, unable to get the government permits needed to start his legitimate import business, he moved back to Ontario with his family.

After 1990, DeRosa was supported financially by his younger brother.

While he did not have a criminal record, Bob DeRosa did have an aggressive way of talking. His cousin would later say that, ever since he was five years old, Bob had a temper and that he "rants and then he doesn't — he would never hurt anybody that I am aware of." Bob's mother would say of her oldest son, "When he is angry and maybe he has been drinking a bit, he sounds like he's going to kill somebody, but he's not even able to kill a fly when he drinks."

Bob DeRosa had a firearms license and three registered firearms: a Glock .40 calibre pistol, a Mossberg pump-action shotgun and a Savage Arms Mark II .22 calibre rifle. He told female members of his family that he needed the guns because he lived near a forest and might be attacked by a wild animal, giving the example of a raccoon.

Bob DeRosa often told people he was a co-owner of the Barrie property. That was not true; he was not rich and did not even own the small bison farm in Phelpston, Ontario, where he lived with his wife and three sons — it was owned by a corporation controlled by his younger and more successful brother.

In late 2001, Bob started working for Vincent at the Molson plant. The older brother would tell people he was managing a project there called Aurora Beverages, which bottled water. This bottling company had filters and other machinery but was never fully operational. A lot of money and much of Vincent's energy was devoted to the scheme, which was doomed after Pepsi and Nestlé entered the market and sold water at prices too low for Aurora to compete. "I never saw any water bottled there," DiCicco later said.

Bob DeRosa was the manager of another company leasing space in the building — National Roasters. Every week (according to McGee) Bob received a cash payment of $3,000 to $4,000 from his younger brother.

After Bleich was fired, DiCicco stopped working security at the front gate and helped with grow-op logistics. Whenever a crop of cannabis had been harvested, dried and trimmed, a man known to DiCicco only as "the Preacher" would arrive at the Molson building to take it away. A co-worker later said the Preacher was "a recovering alcoholic. He'd go on benders, disappear for a week. Also into cocaine." The Preacher would return to Barrie, bearing several envelopes of money for DiCicco. One bundle of cash would total $17,500. DiCicco would deposit this money into his Barrie Good Fish account at Toronto-Dominion Bank, then write a check for the same amount to the company owned by Vincent DeRosa — supposedly, this was the rent paid by Barrie Good Fish for its space in the building. DiCicco would hand these checks to Bob DeRosa. In this way, Dolic used DiCicco to pay $17,500 every month in rent for the Ontario Pallet grow op.

Another envelope of cash from the Preacher would total between $15,000 and $20,000. This was "the float," which DiCicco used to buy groceries, cigarettes and takeout food for the people who lived and worked in the grow op. DiCicco was also responsible for renting the large metal bins used to store garbage from the grow op — empty chemical containers, old potting soil, the worthless roots and stalks of cannabis plants, etc. — until the incriminating evidence could be disposed of off-site.

Later, when police raided DiCicco's home in the old beer store, they found a handwritten note from a grow-op manager that read:

Mike,

I need from the hydro store [Hydroponics Gardens, Mississauga,
Ontario] as soon as possible

2 boxes of [soil] cubes

1 box of trays

1 box of trays with holes

3 large syringes (140 ml)

On another occasion, DiCicco was sent to buy $4,000 worth of electrical wire. And a sales clerk at a Barrie electrical-supply store would later remember DiCicco coming in to buy, with cash, 12 Canarm high-velocity fans in the fall of 2003.

DiCicco would also receive his own pay from the Preacher. His income was based on how much cannabis was produced and what price Dolic sold it for. His monthly payments generally totaled $15,000, or about $180,000 a year.

As "chief engineer" for the property, DiCicco's official annual salary from Vincent DeRosa's company was $24,000. Once the grow op was running, Dolic and Freeman made a deal with Bob DeRosa. Freeman told DiCicco to start paying the money from his regular salary to Bob. DiCicco didn't understand this arrangement but agreed to it. So when DiCicco got his weekly $500 check from Vincent's company, he would take it to the bank and cash the check. Then he would give the cash to Bob. This was a strange arrangement, DiCicco felt, but he was making lots of money and did not complain.

When not working, DiCicco liked to relax at his home in the old beer store. He drank beer, Molson Canadian being his brand of choice. He owned movies on DVD, such as *Gangs of New York* and *Hustler's Barely Legal*. And he kept a big baggie of cannabis from the nearby grow op at his home. Sometimes he would leave the property to visit his woman in Toronto.

Eventually, much of the old Molson building would be rented out to legitimate businesses. When DiCicco worked his shift at the guardhouse, most of the traffic would be for Kuni, a car-parts outfit connected to Honda. There were several trucking companies: First Team Transport, Karlea Transport, Streamline Transport, First Team Transport, Smitty's Transport and two independent truckers. Two small beer-makers — Flying Monkey Craft Brewery and Simcoe Steam Brewing — also rented storage space at the former Molson brewery. The owner of Simcoe Steam Brewing Company also sold the soggy leftover grains from his brewery to Bob DeRosa, who fed it to his bison.

By the end, up to 200 people worked at the 12 companies leasing space on the property — including several companies linked to the DeRosas and managed by Bob DeRosa.

Briefing

The first evidence of human cannabis use is from Central Europe and China, 7,000 years ago.

In 1606, cannabis was first grown by Europeans in the land that would later become Canada.

Cannabis — also called hemp and good for making ropes for sailboats — was legal in British North America for many centuries; the government paid cash rewards to farmers for growing cannabis and published booklets on the most effective cannabis-farming methods.

In 1922, things changed in Canada when Emily Murphy — an Albertan who was Canada's first female judge — published a book on drugs and ethnicity called *The Black Candle*. She wrote:

> Persons using this narcotic [cannabis] smoke the dried leaves
> of the plant, which has the effect of driving them completely
> insane. The addict loses all sense of moral responsibility. Addicts
> to this drug, while under its influence, are immune to pain
> and could be severely injured without having any realization
> of their condition . . . [Cannabis addicts] become raving
> lunatics and are liable to kill or indulge in any form of violence
> to other persons using the most savage methods of cruelty
> . . . Their mentality is that of idiots. If this drug is indulged in to
> any great extent, it ends in the untimely death of the addict
> . . . The drug is used for the purpose of inducing pleasurable
> motor excitement and hallucinations which are commonly
> sexual in character among Eastern races . . . Many Negroes
> are law-abiding and altogether estiminable, but contrariwise,
> many are obstinately wicked persons, earning their livelihood
> as freeranging pedlars of poisonous drugs . . . This weed of

madness . . . [will] bring about the degeneracy of the
white race . . .

Murphy's book was very influential. In 1923, the Canadian government made cannabis illegal. South of the border, New York State had started restricting cannabis in 1914. Other U.S. states would follow New York's lead over the next two decades. The U.S. federal government criminalized cannabis in 1937.

 Things Fall Apart

"Cops are parked outside and we went and removed the junk, eh."
— Jeff DaSilva

In a big building on an industrial strip in St. Catharines, near Lake Ontario and a Canadian Tire outlet, Glenn Day did some construction work at a Dolic-funded grow op. The property was owned by a corporation controlled by Vincent DeRosa, and his brother Bob, who falsely claimed to co-own it, acted as landlord. The place was called Ssonix, after a waste-disposal company that rented most of the building. Bob had once owned the waste-disposal company, but, because of financial difficulties, had sold it to Vincent.

Soon after making rental arrangements with Bob DeRosa, Dolic, Freeman, DaSilva and Day went to St. Catharines, where Dolic explained what kind of grow up he wanted built. Freeman, who lived in nearby Niagara Falls with his wife and four daughters, was the "main guy on-site," playing the same role at Ssonix that Robert Bleich had played at Molson. Unlike at the Molson plant, where electricity was paid for, DaSilva installed an electrical bypass at Ssonix and the plants fed on stolen power.

During construction, Day was fired. "We were there, working," he later recalled. "I lost the fucking pump cart I had rented. I rented a bunch of shit over there and then they told me they didn't want me there. Dan [Dolic] told me — he says, 'Don't go back there.' I said, 'Well, whatever. I don't give a fuck.'"

That wasn't the end of the setbacks at Ssonix. DaSilva described knocking down a wall there: "We pull it with the forklift and then it wasn't going so we nudged it a bit on the bottom and then pulled it back with the forklift and it just fucking came down like a fucking — We pulled it with a chain and it fucking just cleared the forklift at the front . . . We had to wait until the dust settled to see if everybody was still there." They also had water problems, at one point having to install a pool in the basement to store the overflow.

Disaster struck the Ssonix grow op before it really got started. Toward the end of June 2003, an environmental enforcement officer for the Region of Niagara named Aarne Salojarvi began an investigation into how oil was getting into the industrial strip's sewage system. Salojarvi showed up at the Ssonix property and climbed down a manhole outside the building, where he noticed something odd — not the oil that he was looking for, but water, mysteriously flowing from the Ssonix building into the sewer pipe. He decided to investigate the source of the water.

Salojarvi phoned the Ssonix general manager, who said there had not been any waste treated by Ssonix at the building for months; he didn't know what could be leaking water. He said that space in the St. Catharines building was being rented by someone else, but he didn't know who and he didn't have keys to all of the units. The manager told Salojarvi that the contact person was Ssonix president Vincent DeRosa.

The next day, the environmental enforcement officer returned to the Ssonix property. He met the manager, who told him the new owner of the property was a man named Fred, but the manager did not have Fred's number — he'd call Vincent DeRosa to get it.

Twenty-eight minutes after Salojarvi left the property, he got a phone call from Fred Freeman, who said he worked for the property's owner. That was a lie; however, Freeman was in negotiations with Vincent DeRosa to buy the property — negotiations that would later fall apart. Freeman said the building was undergoing construction to become a factory for Jacuzzi whirlpool baths, and a broken water heater and toilet had caused the flow of water into the sewer. Salojarvi said he might need to inspect the building's unit 6, where the water heater was located.

A week or so later, Salojarvi showed up at the Ssonix property. When he knocked on the door of unit 6, a man with a strong Quebecois accent spoke briefly with him, refusing to let him in. Salojarvi called the number Freeman had left and spoke to the apparent owner of the building, asking to enter the building to inspect. The man on the phone was reluctant, complaining that he was being picked on. He said Salojarvi would have to talk with Freeman about access. Salojarvi again left the property.

The next day, the Ssonix general manager phoned the inspector, saying he now had the keys. Salojarvi drove over, and when they entered unit 6, he saw a kitchen with new appliances, including a fridge full of food. In a garage area, he found a large number of electrical supplies and tools, and in another room, a large quantity of wiring and an electrical panel. The area had been renovated to create two floors. Salojarvi went up to the second floor and found a grow op, with many small cannabis plants. He went back outside and phoned the Niagara Regional Police. While waiting for the police to arrive, the Ssonix general manager went to his office and made some phone calls.

Alerted about the crisis, DaSilva and a few of his tradesmen sneaked into unit 6, undetected, and got to work. They grabbed all the cloned babies and took them out a back door into a field behind the building. DaSilva later recalled, "Cops are parked outside and we went and removed the junk, eh."

A police officer accompanied Salojarvi for the rest of the environmental inspection. They found three large grow rooms, with

200 high-intensity lights and sophisticated lighting and ventilation systems. The grow rooms contained black plastic pots, soil, fertilizer and hydrogen peroxide (to kill mold, fungi and bacteria). But no plants. There were also two drying rooms and a baby room. The inspectors noted that the construction seemed recent, but no people were seen and there was no sign the grow op had ever been used.

Looking around in back of the building, the police officers sat down near where DaSilva had hidden the babies, but they didn't notice them.

That night, with an officer sitting in a cruiser parked in front, DaSilva sneaked into the Ssonix building again to disconnect the electrical bypass, so nobody would get charged with theft of power. As it turned out, nobody would ever be charged with anything over the short-lived Ssonix grow op.

. . . .

Dinner at a steakhouse, one night in 2003.

At the table were Dolic, Freeman, DaSilva, Day and a Dolic associate nicknamed "Tripper." Tripper was in his late 30s, big and tall, bald. Bleich did not like him. DaSilva was meeting Tripper for the first time. They were there to talk about a grow op planned for Oro, a rural town just north of Barrie, in a strip mall managed by Bob DeRosa and owned by a company controlled by Vincent. The area for the grow op was rented by a front company that supposedly made mattresses. The lease was signed for the front company by a young member of Dolic's gang who was paid 5 percent of the profit to be the legal fall guy or patsy. Other, apparently legitimate, businesses in the strip mall included a bailiff's office and a Canada Post outlet.

Dolic had hired Tripper to build the Oro grow op. He had invested $100,000 so far and had called this meeting in frustration over Tripper taking too long. All Tripper had completed so far were the living quarters. Dolic told Tripper he was no longer in charge of construction at Oro. DaSilva would take over, with Day's help, and get it built in reasonable time. DaSilva would get $200,000 (100 candles at $2,000 each) to finish the job. Tripper was not pleased about losing the construction contract.

When DaSilva got to the Oro site, he realized that Tripper's construction crew had messed up, cutting an exhaust hole in the wrong place. DaSilva and Day built the second floor of the Oro grow op and a wall to hide it. Day got cash from DaSilva to buy drywall and other supplies at a Home Depot, and he booked hotel rooms for DaSilva and his crew, in Barrie, right beside Highway 400.

The Oro project took DaSilva, Day and two electricians from Montreal over two months to wire. They spent a lot of time fastening timers and ballasts to pieces of plywood. As at the Molson plant, they did not install an electrical bypass — the grow op's energy would be legitimately bought. DaSilva had to install a pool for flooding and drill a well for water shortages.

During construction at Oro, Dolic introduced Day to Bob DeRosa, who claimed to co-own both Oro and the Molson buildings. Bob did two walk-through inspections. On a third walk-through, after the Oro grow op had started operation, Bob saw some plants growing in pots of soil; he phoned Dolic to complain of the smell, and Dolic had Day deal with it. Day hung up some more drywall to cut down the smell.

On at least two occasions during the construction of the Oro grow op, Bob DeRosa got mad at delivery people and yelled at them. Later, when Bob DeRosa's circumstances were very different, these outbursts would come back to haunt him: the delivery men would remember him.

When the Oro grow op was operating, Bob DeRosa complained about the high cost of the electricity. So Dolic handed Day $18,000 cash in a Purolator bag, which Day took directly to DeRosa, to satisfy the loud and aggressive property manager.

The Oro grow op was only live for two or three months before a big disaster. According to Dolic, Tripper had enlisted a group of hoodlums to get revenge for his firing. On January 8, 2004, Tripper's thugs — carrying firearms and wearing identical balaclava face masks and boots — burst into the grow op, frightening the growers and trimmers. The masked men, who were later described as acting like cops or bikers, pointed their guns at Dolic's terrified employees and robbed the place. As Tripper's thugs left Oro with the stolen salad, one taunted Dolic's workers that the Barrie grow op was going to be "ratted out!"

That was not an empty threat. An OPP officer later said that the informant who had told them about Molson — Tripper, according to Dolic — had, over the past decade, informed on other drug dealers 20 times.

. . . .

December 2003.

A Christmas party in the Molson Plant's Canadiana Room was attended by employees of Fercan, building tenants, property inspectors for the City of Barrie, staff of the Barrie Fire Department, staff of the electricity company and Bob DeRosa.

Shortly after this party, the Canadiana Room would be invaded and trashed by armed, shouting men: police officers.

Briefing

Some of the Barrie police officers involved in the 2004 raid:

Inspectors Bruce Carlson, Jim Farrell

Staff Sergeants Steve Bishop, Dave Hossack, P. McGarry

Sergeants R. Allen, D. Berrialt, Rob Burke, Tim Conroy, Greer, M. Hartshorn, Mark Holder, Dave Jones, N. Meech, D. Partridge, Mark Shaffer, Tom Sinclair, Gord Spears, D. Taylor, D. Vaillancourt, S. Wilson

Constables C. Alton, T. Armstrong, Kevin Beirus, Bernard, D. Bosch, Greg Brickell, J. Brooks, K. Caddell, B. Carleton, Chris Castonguay, Chorley, L. Conley, G. Crooks, Crosby, M. Deason, Peter Dewsnap, D. Donald, Jason Dorian, R. Dow, Wayne Dufour, J. Eden, Fearon, K. Franke, Glen Furlong, Bill Gigg, Dave Goodbrand, M. Gould, William Grant, M. Hale, B. Haynes, J. Heard, Doug Henderson, T. Higgins, Roxanne Hodgins, M. Horne, Ian Hughes, S. Hutchinson, Richard Johnson, P. Kellachan, Mark Kennie, P. Kluszcznski, John Lamont, Ted Lunstead, C. Manna, T. Marsh, Matthew Marshall, Cameron McCrea, Tony McLarty, Kevin McLean, R. McLeod, McRae, S. Middleton, John Mills, Carl Moore, Munro, C. Nicholls, O'Donohue, Ouellette, Mel Palma, John Parcells, C. Parrish, J. Peters, C. Phillips, E. Ramsey, Brian Read, Reiley, R. Riddell, R. Ritcher, Rye, E. Savoie, D. Schaly, J. Schefter, Rob Scott, B. Shultz, J. Stamp, N. Towns, D. Van Schubert, Velema, J. Watt, Duncan Way, R. Wentzell, J. Westcott, L. White, L. Wisotski, Jim Yon.

Some of the Ontario Provincial Police and other officers involved in the 2004 raid:

Inspector J. Wilkinson

Staff Sergeants Rick Barnum, Cross, G. Edwards, Latouf, R. Thompson

Sergeants K. Anderson, R. Brennan, Rod Carscallon, Jamie Ciotka, G. Depratto, K. Hunter, L. Kienapple, M. Milner, Pearson, G. Speers, L. Woodman

Constables M. Ahrens, J. Aitkenhead, Robert Allen, S. Anthony, I. Austin, M. Baker, D. Banks, S. Barnstaple, K. Barnum, M. Beauchesne, Mike Bednarcyzk (alias: "Bedrock"), Brent Bergeron, H. Bowden, P. Browne, G. Buffett, J. Buligan, K. Butler, S. Cartwright, L. Childs, Chris, D. Collins, H. Collins, R. Conn, S. Connor, J. Cooper, P. Coulis, Croker, T. Cuff, K. Daniels-Griffis, A. Debrouwer, M. Devries, Dick, P. Does, Doldernan, J. Dorion, J. Dudinski, Rick Dupuis, J. Eden, S. El-Amad, D. Epp, G. Ewald, Farrell, A. Ferrao, D. Fitzgerald, K. Fitzgerald, S. Floyd, Foss, G. Furlong, M. Gauthier, K. German, J. Gillespie, Goobie, M. Groleau, S. Haight, R. Hanicec, Heinemann, C. Inman, J. Irvine, M. James, B. Jarvis, P. Jervis, D. Jones, Kaiser, Kelly, Kelsall, W. King, J. Kinsella, M. Knox, Kummer, M. Kurkimaki, T. Kylyruik, Landerville, Dave Light, J. Macdonald, S. Macdonald, P. Mackey, B. Macmurchy, Macphail, S. Macphie, Manca, K. Manley, P. Marchand, Marino, W. Martin, S. McLeod, T. McLeod, B. McRoberts, L. Mendoza, D. Milne, M. Mobbs, J. Mortimer, Baldo Nuccio, J. Oke, S. O'Neil, Parker, M. Parsons, Penrose, Powers, A. Quemby, Quesnelle, Quinn, J. Ramsey, P. Robinson, Roco, Ruggles, Sakolo, J. Sanders, C. Sharland, Schely, Schlorff, J. Schuett, J. Scott, Shantz, Semple, J. Spence, M. Stacey, C. Stewart, S. Stewart, D. Strickler, A. Tait, G. Tardiff, B. Thomas, T. Thompson, Dan Tucker, H. Van Hees, Van Dusen, A. Waddington, Rusty Watson, Weirsema, R. Wells, G. Wheeler, B. Winter, J. Yen, Zapotoczny, S. Zivanov, M. Zwarun.

# The Raid

"We got it!"
— An officer at the Molson building raid

On Friday, January 9, 2004, at 2:55 p.m., Tripper contacted Barrie Constable Peter Dewsnap at police headquarters at 20 Rose Street. He told Dewsnap that a grow op in the Molson building was located "at south of plant . . . by the brewing vats," that police would find "1,000 grow lites" and that people were being brought in to "process" (trim) the product, bringing the total number of people in the grow op to 40. Tripper said a crop would be harvested the next day.

Barrie Police decided to act fast, fearing that waiting until after the harvest was done could lead to a loss of evidence and opportunities to make arrests. At 3:17 p.m., Dewsnap contacted Barrie Hydro and asked for information about electricity usage at the old Molson factory. He learned that electricity usage had recently spiked and water usage had declined significantly.

At 3:40 p.m., according to his handwritten notes, OPP Constable Dan Tucker did a "perimeter drive by of the plant located at 1 Big Bay Point Road." Half an hour later, OPP Constable Brent Bergeron called the Barrie Fire Department and had them fax over a floor plan of the Molson building and a partial list of its occupants: a "bottling plant," a "trucking company," a "storage area" and a "fish hatchery."

At 4:37 p.m., according to his handwritten notes, Barrie Police Constable Rob Scott "attends the Land Registry office and obtains a copy of the land registry documents for the plant at 1 Big Bay Point Road." Then Bergeron called the Barrie city planning department; a helicopter was sent to photograph the Molson building and an OPP officer got to work on a media release.

· · · · · · ·

OPP Constable Michael Bednarcyzk was based in Barrie. He was trim, five-foot-nine, with shoulder-length hair and a narrow, handsome face. He had been a police officer for eight years. On the afternoon of January 9, at 4:18 p.m., Bednarcyzk's sergeant told him of the grow-op tip (not revealing the identity of the informant) and that they were working on a search warrant for the place. According to Bednarcyzk's handwritten investigation notes, his sergeant told him to go "maintain eye on access point to Molson plant — make des[cription] of vehicles, specifically vehicles that could be used to transport large amounts of people to/from plant." After Tucker's drive-by, Bednarcyzk was the second police officer to do surveillance of the suspected grow op.

To the east of the property — separated by a huge empty field — was a gardening center and tree nursery, where Bednarcyzk pulled into the snow-covered parking lot. He parked his unmarked vehicle there at 5:43 p.m., about 500 yards away. He could see the building well from here, especially when he used binoculars. When it started to get dark, Bednarcyzk could still see well, by the lights of the property's gatehouse and the bright lights over the Molson parking lot. He saw many trucks going in and out, and noted that the snow around the plant was covered with tire tracks.

It was very cold — about -22 Fahrenheit — so he had to leave his engine on to heat the car, causing a cloud of exhaust to accumulate behind the vehicle and drift with the wind, visible from afar. He sat there, watching the occasional traffic at the Molson property, for almost five hours. He would later be joined by other surveillance officers from both Barrie Police and the OPP.

At 7:30 p.m., the officers watching the Molson property saw a cube van drive out, followed by a red and silver pickup truck. Police tried to stop the cube van, which was registered to Multi Brand Food Corporation, owner of National Roasters. The driver of the van took a while to respond to the flashing lights and sirens behind her.

Sitting in the van were Bob DeRosa and driver Hazel Lane,★ his personal assistant and cleaning lady. Constable Bergeron approached DeRosa and showed his badge, identifying himself. DeRosa said, "Drug unit? I don't have any drugs. You can search the van if you want." Bergeron did search, and found nothing but a dryer in the back of the cube van. He apologized and asked DeRosa to come to the police vehicle for more questions.

DeRosa said his brother owned the property and that he helped with rental matters — he didn't have his brother's phone number on him. Bergeron said they were waiting for a warrant to search the building for a grow op, and DeRosa said he "never saw any indication of that." Bergeron took out a floor plan of the building and they went over it together. DeRosa said that the only person in the main building now should be the maintenance man, Larry McGee.

After the police allowed them to drive away, DeRosa told Hazel to phone McGee and tell him that police might be coming into the building. She also phoned the 300-pound guard at the gatehouse with the news.

Bob DeRosa later told his version of the night of the Molson raid: "Seven-thirty at night, we leave the plant in the cube van. Hazel [was] driving . . . They had the highway shut down . . . both ways, eh. The SWAT team, they . . . fucking cut us off, cars coming the other way. You know, they thought the fucking van was full of weed . . . I swear to God, machine guns . . . You remember how cold it was . . . I had fucking just a light jacket on. They had made me freeze outside, honest to God. I got frostbitten outside and Hazel, they fucking roughed her real good trying to get information. I wouldn't give it to them. I said, 'Fuck you. Arrest me. What am I charged with?' He goes, 'Make sure you guys know what you are doing.' He didn't know that I was DeRosa . . . that I owned the fucking plant, me and my brother. They didn't know any of that. When they found out . . . I told them to suck my fucking dick. I said, 'You pieces of shit!' I goes, 'Watch what I'm going to do to you assholes!' . . . They kept me there for two fucking hours . . . on the side of the road . . . They said, 'Listen, do you mind if we —' I wouldn't let them go on the prop[erty] because they . . . need a search warrant. He said, 'Do you mind if we go on the property until we get the search warrant?' I goes, 'No fucking way! You're going nowhere!' I goes, 'When you get the search warrant,' I goes, 'you call me. I'm going to come and let you in.' Listen — the fucking idiots let us go . . . I said, 'Hazel, get on the phone. Call everybody in the plant, let them know there — if the police comes there with a search warrant, they have to let them in' . . . The security guy . . . calls me back and says, 'What do you want me to do?' I goes, 'Einstein, what do you think you're going to do? They're coming with a search warrant! . . . You've got to let them in . . . What are you going to do, fight them? Shoot them? Be a gentleman!'"

Word of the impending search warrant made it to Michael DiCicco, living with a cat named Bubbas in the red-brick building just north of the brewery that had once been a drive-through beer store. DiCicco passed on the warning to one manager, Denis Hould, and tried to contact the Ontario Pallet manager, Scott Walker, but Walker's phones were dead, so he and his crew missed the warning.

At 8:21 p.m., Bednarcyzk noted, he was contacted by Sergeant Jamie Ciotka, who "adv[ised] to keep an eye for activity, [the people in the] plant may be aware of police presence . . . Ciotka also request[ed] I check west side of plant for activity, specifically in the area of silos at S/W corner of plant — info that grow is located at south end."

Bednarcyzk went for a drive, and parked his unmarked car at the shoulder of Highway 400, just to the southwest of the target property. At 9:16 p.m., he noted "a bright light" shining up from skylight windows at the tops of two of the three big silos. The rest of the building was dark.

Bednarcyzk called in a report about the mysterious light, which was used to support the search warrant application being prepared for a judge's signature. The constable thought it strange for skylight windows to be open on a -22 Fahrenheit night. (The source of this "bright light," also described in police records as "powerful and intense," was never determined.) He drove back to the gardening center nursery.

At 9:56 p.m., Bednarcyzk and the other officers at the freezing-cold garden center lot saw a 2002 maroon Dodge minivan, its roof covered with snow, go out of the plant. It was driven by a man described by police as "a white male in his mid 40s with a medium build, salt-and-pepper hair, a goatee, big nose and prescription glasses."

It was Hould, who later said, "I got the phone call and then I got my whole crew together and got everybody out." There was at least one unseen passenger inside the maroon minivan, the police surveillance noted — they did not know that Hould was driving six crouching gardeners. Noticing the police behind him, Hould drove the minivan — whose ownership was later traced to his wife — east on Big Bay Point Road, then south on Bayview and west on Molson Park Drive, passing over Highway 400. He stopped at a Tim Hortons, then turned around and went back east on Molson Park Drive. The pursuing Barrie Police officer was told by a sergeant not to stop the van, to "let it run." Hould turned onto Highway 400 southbound, losing the police and getting his crew clean away.

. . . .

Earlier in the evening, Robert Bleich had been sitting with Scott Walker inside a warm Kelsey's restaurant in Barrie, enjoying a tasty dinner. Even though he had been fired for his "conflict of interest," Bleich had remained friends with Walker and was free to visit the grow op. The two men had enjoyed sizzling fajitas and a couple of cold beers.

They left Kelsey's and got into Bleich's brown minivan and drove south down Highway 400, toward Walker's workplace. When they pulled into the Molson property, the guard at the gatehouse said to Walker, "We've been trying to get hold of you all night!" (Walker owned several phones but, he now discovered, he had let all their batteries die.) The guard told them about the phone call from Bob DeRosa.

Bleich and Walker could have easily turned around and driven away. If they'd just tried to escape the police trap, they probably would have slipped out, like Hould and his crew.

But they didn't. Instead, they tried to be heroes.

Looking east across the fields to the garden center parking lot, Bleich recalled, "we could see cars sitting outside. They had their exhaust on because it was cold, they needed heat at the garden center. So we knew something was going down. We drove . . . to the door. Walker went in. Walker came out with the others. [Gardeners] Rayne Sauve and Craig Walker got in the minivan. [Other gardeners climbed into a pickup truck and another van. At 9:56 p.m.] we drove out in a little convoy, with me driving in front. Turned left on Big Bay Road. The plan was to drop them off at a hotel somehow. We made it down the hill, took a left, then a right. It was about five minutes. I didn't notice that we were being followed. [The van's windows were foggy.] We got to Dunlop and [Tiffin] street. There was a red light and a red car in front of me, waiting. As I started to drive around this car, seven to eight cop cars, 15 to 20 cops. I was smoking a cigarette. The cops came at us from all directions. There were a couple of big guns pointed at us — M16-type rifles. Every car had four to five cops in it. A cop had a 9 mm gun pointed in the crack of my window. His hands were shaking, he was nervous. We got cuffed and they did a search, emptied out our pockets. They put us in a van that pulled up and we went to downtown Barrie. As we went into the station one by one, we were strip-searched and put into individual cells. It was the coldest night of the year — minus 30 — and we were all freezing. It was cold in the police station, coldest in the cells . . ."

The gardeners reeked. It was "a strong odor of marijuana . . . [a] skunky smell similar to that of growing plants," according to Sergeant Jamie Ciotka; the "pungent odor of weed," according to Constable Bill Gigg. Constable Doug Henderson described it as the "extreme odor of fresh marijuana on him. Very obvious that male had just come from an area where fresh marijuana had been."

A search of the arrested men and the three vehicles turned up thousands of dollars in cash and many cell phones; police would later search the contact lists and call histories of each phone, gathering a lot of useful information.

Also found on the arrested men were large amounts of cannabis flowers, plus relatively small quantities of Percocet, cannabis oil and a single, tiny ecstasy pill marked with a kangaroo symbol. One gardener had a small bag of seven grams of crack cocaine hidden inside his boxers.

· · · · · · ·

Barrie police gathered at a staging area in the parking lot of a Radio Shack on Bayview Street near the Molson property, waiting for permission to enter. (The staging area was later moved to the parking lot of a nearby Coca-Cola bottling plant.)

Other officers waited at the McDonald's on Fairview Road, awaiting orders to block traffic from approaching the Molson property.

The search warrant application was signed by a judge at 11:21 p.m., authorizing the raid.

· · · · · · ·

At 12:05 a.m., Bednarcyzk noted, "Obs[erved] convoy of police veh[icles] from Bayview, north of BBP [Big Bay Point], enter upon property using BBP entrance."

At 12:07 a.m., two Barrie Police officers — Sergeant Dave Jones and Constable Greg Brickell — went onto the Molson land and to the guardhouse. They arrested the security guard there for possession of drugs (he actually didn't have drugs on him and would later be released without charge).

Then about 30 heavily armed and armored officers of the Barrie Emergency Response Unit penetrated the Molson property, toward the main building, and 20 or so more ERU officers arrived, working with the OPP in setting up a perimeter. Some officers were in uniform, others were plainclothes. Concerned about booby traps, police also called in bomb-sniffing dogs.

OPP officers from Toronto, Odessa, Kingston, London, Midland, Belleville, Oshawa and St. Catharines arrived in stages and joined in the search or securing the building, raising the number of officers at the property to more than 100. Some had been instructed to arrive wearing green uniforms and bulletproof vests. In addition to their Glock-style pistols, all carried assault rifles; some had the .223 Ruger, others had the C8 — a shorter-barreled variation of the C7 used by the Canadian forces, with a killing range of a quarter-mile. A few officers from the Niagara Regional Police Morality Unit also arrived.

Heavy weapons held at the ready, armored police officers of the Tactics and Rescue Unit performed what one of them described as a "dynamic entry" — smashing an exterior door with sledgehammers. "The Tactics and Rescue Unit rarely uses doorways [in a normal, non-dynamic way]," Bednarcyzk would later testify.

The door down, a TRU officer yelled, "Police! Search warrant!" After a pause, the police burst in. At first, they found nothing drug-related: just the interior of a large, rundown, dirty building lit in places by overhead fluorescent lights, parts of it leased to different businesses. Heading to the area that Tripper had told Constable Dewsnap about, the fermentation area leased by Barrie Good Fish, the TRU moved slowly and methodically, room by room, knocking doors off hinges and puncturing holes in walls.

One of them noted, "Began search of plant in question. Extremely large in area — Searched office area + centre area of plant. Unable to locate marijuana plants."

Eventually, they found their way blocked by a large metal freezer-style door that was locked. Instead of immediately trying to breach this door, the officers decided to go back outside and try one of the fermentation area's exterior doors. Walking on the snowy concrete between rows of tall, vertical, metal tanks, they approached a white-painted metal door at the extreme southeast of the building. At 1:02 in the morning of January 10, they breached this exterior door with a sledgehammer and went in, finding bags of Pro-Mix soil, boxes of used HID bulbs, gardening tools, empty butane cans, bamboo stakes and other suspicious items. Exploring further, the tactical officers found 23 beer tanks wired up and attached to big air conditioners.

Nearby, a TV had been left on, playing a porn video, as if someone had left in a big hurry. The porn was playing in the background when the officers opened up the hole at the front of one of the tanks. Looking in, they were dazzled by the brilliant bulbs and the hundreds of big, swaying breaches of the federal Controlled Drugs and Substances Act.

One officer radioed his commander at the Coca-Cola staging area: "We got it!"

Most of the officers were too big in the shoulders to squeeze inside the tank, but Bednarcyzk was slight enough in build to get in. He noted, "Hundreds of cannabis marijuana plants growing in a vat, using HID lights, sophisticated vent. system using tank openings, plastic barrels to store water & chemicals — rows of vats w[ith] hundreds of plants per vat — strong odor of cannabis marijuana . . . apparent that growers are very knowledgable."

Another officer wrote, "Enormity of grow 'house' hard to put into words — unbelievable!!" while another later noted, "Most sophisticated grow operation ever seen."

By the amazing, jungle-jammed vats, an officer sliced open the side of a full orange garbage bag. Dried cannabis flowers avalanched out.

．　．　．　．　．　．　．

While the Tactics and Rescue Unit was finding more forbidden salad, other detachments of police officers were investigating the rest of the property.

At the time, a husband and wife — co-owners of a small trucking company that rented indoor parking space from Vincent DeRosa — and their friend were sitting by their trucks in the southeast corner of the building, with a little pet dog, drinking beer. A large team of TRU officers with C8 assault rifles and body armor surrounded the truckers and handcuffed them. At first, the startled truckers thought it was about their open bottles of beer.

Elsewhere on the property, another trucker was detained by police. Under questioning, he confessed that he had recently picked up a load of carrots from the Holland Marsh area near Newmarket and had conveyed them, for personal profit, to a carrot dealer in Barrie.

When the London tactical OPP unit later tried to leave the site, they found that the battery of their bomb truck had frozen and the engine wouldn't start. The bomb truck was towed to the Barrie police station for repair.

Briefing

Like all living things, the cannabis plant contains DNA — a genetic code, twisted into every cell, that guides its growth.

In the cannabis industry, genetic technology is used in two main ways:

One: by law enforcement, to analyze the DNA of seized plants. There are other methods that can determine whether or not a substance is cannabis — e.g., chemical spot tests, chromatography and examination though a microscope — but DNA analysis is superior, as it can show the relationship between different samples of cannabis, in the same way that human DNA analysis can show family relationships between people.

Two: by cannabis farmers, to grow new kinds of cannabis. By inserting snippets of foreign DNA into cannabis, growers can improve plants in radical ways not possible by traditional breeding — to grow faster, to survive herbicides, to repel bugs, to make a particular blend of psychoactive chemicals, to glow in the dark, etc. Much of the food eaten by North Americans (especially corn and soy) is genetically modified, containing the DNA of other organisms (sometimes from non-plant species, like scorpions or jellyfish). Some in the cannabis industry want to follow that path. Are consumers ready for Frankenstein weed?

Into the Labyrinth

"Keep eye for hidden walls + secret doors."
— An officer at the Molson building raid

At eight the next morning, a Barrie Police sergeant went to the Canadiana Room, a large area just south of the fermentation tanks, now used as the office for several DeRosa companies. The fancy-looking room had a fireplace, mahogany beams and a high ceiling; an Emergency Response officer from Bolton would later describe it as a "ritzy office." The Canadiana Room — which looked as if it had been designed by an advertising agency — was where Molson's guests had once been given free beer at the end of a tour.

The sergeant spoke to one of Bob DeRosa's assistant property managers, telling him that nobody would be able to access their vehicles on the property. The assistant manager told the officer that would be a big inconvenience for the tenant trucking companies, with their "just in time" delivery schedules. The sergeant was sympathetic but would not change his position.

Bob DeRosa was present for this conversation, but said nothing. He was asleep at a desk during the entire OPP visit. The assistant manager had not been able to wake him up.

·　·　·　·　·　·

When Constable Bednarcyzk left at 2:00 a.m. to get some sleep, the Barrie Good Fish grow tanks were the only drug-cultivation spots the police had yet found. The intensive search continued, officers marking off areas they'd examined with strips of flagging tape. The building was such a bewildering labyrinth that — without tape — officers would have had a hard time knowing what had and had not been searched. "Very confusing inside," an officer noted.

When Bednarcyzk returned the next afternoon, he learned that more cryptic and taboo horticulture had been found in the old beer factory. Eventually, police would uncover four separate cannabis-growing areas inside the massive complex.

At 1:00 p.m. on Saturday, January 10 — 13 hours after finding the first plants at Barrie Good Fish, 10 minutes before the first press release went out — the police found what they would call "grow area #2" — the four big rooms that Bleich and DaSilva had built in the area leased by Ontario Pallet. Bleich later said proudly, "They took a long time to find our . . . side . . . It took them like 16 hours . . . They smashed a hole through one of the windows or something in the bedrooms."

The police officers found the packaging room, with bags of flowers and shake, and a digital scale left on — its red LED display inexplicably flashing "6" over and over.

The common room was still decorated for Christmas: dangling strands of gold tinsel, a big white sign that read *Xmas* and wires full of glittering, multicolored lights. Police found Christmas cards to grow-op workers, some signed *Granny & Grandpa* or *Mom* or *Mom and Ralph* or *Grandma R.* Other paperwork that workers left behind included family court documents, phone bills, Workplace Safety and Insurance correspondence, income tax documents, banking papers, hospital records, a probation and parole calendar, a letter from Mohawk College, real estate listings, checks, receipts, pay stubs, bills from the 407 toll highway, a bus transfer, a census form, drug prescriptions, an

Old West calendar, a Notice of Appearance regarding a charge of possession of cannabis, a summons for driving while suspended, a season's pass to Canada's Wonderland, a prescription pill bottle from Pharmasave Drugstore in Barrie with *Davorka Pelikan* on the label, a personal letter written to Fred Freeman, a Home Depot receipt in Hould's name, a well-drawn pencil sketch of a beast signed by the 300-pound gatehouse guard, a Future Shop receipt, a Blockbuster Video membership in Tripper's name, six address books with Dolic's phone number and other documents of interest to police.

In Walker's porn-saturated bedroom, the monitor for the hidden video cameras in the clipping room had been left on. By his bed, police found a copy of Jorge Cervantes' classic agriculture guide, *The Indoor Marijuana Grower's Bible*. Officers also seized several computers from the premises and would later copy their hard drives.

When police entered the grow rooms — which had been hidden in order to frustrate just such a police exploration — the officers found that a stereo there had been left on with loud music blasting from the speakers. The officers left the music on in the background as they examined the rows of vegetation.

There were no signs that anybody had ever built pallets at Ontario Pallet, just as police found nothing related to fish at Barrie Good Fish. They did find receipts there from Barrie Hydro — dated January 7, 2004 — showing payment of an electricity bill for $80,388.12.

The third grow op the police discovered — after those at Barrie Good Fish and Ontario Pallet — was a small one hidden in an office being used as an apartment by handyman Larry McGee. The police smashed the glass at the top of his door to get in. They arrested McGee, who claimed he'd had no idea about cannabis. Lying, he told the police he had stayed away from Barrie Good Fish because Bob DeRosa had said, "Stay the fuck out of Mike [DiCicco's] area!"

In McGee's bedroom, police officers found a big entertainment unit and yanked it from the wall, revealing a large secret room with walls covered in sheets of white plastic and dozens of cannabis plants growing in a hydroponic system, each attached by string to the ceiling for support. (In hydroponic systems, the roots of the plants grow not in soil but water.) Wires and ballasts on the ceiling were connected to the power supply for National Roasters and the grow room's air went out through a vent across the coffee-canner's ceiling.

Police also discovered pesticide sprays and other grow-related equipment in McGee's space. They found porn, lottery tickets, a silver tuba and 47 full two-fours of bottled beer — Canadian, Blue and Coors Light — plus assorted loose bottles of beer and whiskey.

Secret garden #3 was not doing too well when police arrived. "The plants were almost dead," Bednarcyzk would later testify.

The final grow area the police found was in even worse condition. In one of 12 vertical tanks — tanks once used by Molson for storage of beer ingredients — just outside the southeast door, in an area leased by Barrie Good Fish, police found several gardening pots containing dead plants. Bednarcyzk would later testify that someone had apparently tried to grow cannabis here but cold weather and the tank's lack of insulation had led to failure. He called it "an unsuccessful attempt at growing."

. . . .

At the time of the raid, Dolic was in the East Caribbean island of Saint Martin. DiCicco — who had lived in the old drive-through Molson store for two years — was not arrested until hours after the raid started, because the police had to wait for a search warrant for his residence. Until then, DiCicco repeatedly looked out his windows and phoned Dolic in the tropics, describing the situation: "The cops are everywhere! There are more cops here than I've ever seen!" Dolic later said that DiCicco "was my eyes."

At 4:33 p.m. that same Saturday — after taking the air out of the tires on DiCicco's car to prevent it from being used in a getaway — OPP Tactics and Rescue Unit entered the old beer store with a warrant, smashing their way in through a glass door.

"Police! Search warrant!" Constable Marino yelled. "I advise anyone in the residence to place any weapons down and come out to my voice." Getting no response, Marino began a stealth search.

DiCicco stepped out of the building at the other side with his hands held in the air, one of them holding a cigarette, surrendering to an OPP officer. Described later as "polite and cooperative," DiCicco said he had diabetes, so they went in and retrieved his syringe kit and injectable insulin for him. Heart pills were found in one of his pockets. He said he was cold. He was the ninth and last of the men arrested in the 2004 raid.

Bednarcyzk helped search the messy place, noting, "male subj[ect] arrested in bldg — appeared to be flushing dry marijuana down toilet — obs[erved] trail of green plant material from hallway outside bathroom into bathroom, water on floor in bathroom around toilet that appears clogged — empty clear plastic bag w[ith] green dry plant material next to toilet."

When they searched DiCicco, they discovered a key that was later found to open a big blue container outside the building near Barrie Good Fish. Inside the container was a stolen diesel power generator, which would be returned to its owner, in what was surely a heart-touching reunion.

More stolen property was also unearthed, mostly from the Niagara Falls area, including a backhoe, tow motors, cars, snowmobiles and Toro Twister all-terrain vehicles. According to a co-worker, Bob DeRosa was responsible for bringing in the stolen property.

Police raided the mattress store in the Oro strip mall the next day, finding in the basement 1,963 plants, 60 pounds of dried cannabis flowers in boxes on the clipping-room floor, plus many high-intensity candles. The cannabis plants were new seedlings, apparently replacements for those stolen by Tripper's thugs two days earlier. The Oro building's basement was flooded, with four inches of water on the furnace-room floor, from a burst pipe. One of the police's discoveries there was a birdhouse. Hidden inside the birdhouse was a videocamera, connected by coaxial cable to another room; it was apparently used to spy on grow-op workers.

No living people were found at the Oro grow op. But roughly around this time, a dead body was found at the property. According to toxicology studies, the person had died of a drug overdose.

. . . .

Bleich spent his first two nights at the police station in a cold, individual cell. On the third night, he later said, "they put us all together. We huddled together for warmth. We had no shoes. My kidneys hurt from the cold and the floor. Got very little sleep. We didn't talk because it was all videotaped. I called my lawyer [Randall Barrs, who also represented Drago Dolic who had long ago agreed to pay Bleich's legal bills]. Eventually I got bail . . . [It was] a bit inhumane. Four nights with no toothbrush, no soap, freezing on cold cement. It hurts the kidneys, they were frozen. Concrete holds the cold. We couldn't sleep except when we passed out. Spent the whole time huddling."

When he got out on bail, Bleich phoned Budget Rent-A-Car, concerned about having to pay for a van he had rented that was being held by Barrie Police.

. . . .

After Bob DeRosa woke up, he was contacted by the police, who would interview him twice. He denied knowing anything about the growing of cannabis, saying he did not have keys to those areas of the building. Of his younger brother, Bob said, "He's fit to be tied. We don't need this fucking garbage . . . I'm fucking shocked . . . We're not in the drug business. We have too much to lose. We don't want to have nothing to do with drugs . . . I didn't have anything to hide — we don't need to. We never hide anything . . . How do you grow marijuana? I'm not trying to be smart . . . I was raised on a farm. I come from Niagara. My father still has a farm . . . I can't believe that [cannabis farming] was going on in the plant. But it's a big plant."

Larry McGee also claimed ignorance of the grow ops and said he did not have keys to those areas either. (McGee was glad he had always worn gloves when in the grow-op areas, so he did not have to worry about the police finding his fingerprints.)

At the Barrie courthouse one morning, waiting for a bail hearing, a police officer casually asked DiCicco, "How many plants did you have in there?"

"Jeez," DiCicco answered, "I don't know — thousands."

"Like ten thousand?"

"More," DiCicco told the officer.

"Would they be all at the same stage of growth?"

"Dunno. I imagine. They're all different."

Later, that officer asked DiCicco, "Didn't you think someone would get caught, you know, with so many people working in there? Somebody is bound to say something."

"Yeah, you gotta watch out for the bikers," DiCicco said. "If they find out, you know, they'll just come and take over."

"So you were living full-time right in the factory?"

"Well, yeah. But in the old beer-store house."

"You mean the old drive-through beer store?"

"Yeah."

"Why did you live there?"

"It was close to work."

"Where was that?"

DiCicco paused, then said, "Ha ha. You better ask my lawyer."

Soon after that, DiCicco had a heart attack — his third. He went to Barrie's Royal Victoria Hospital for quadruple bypass surgery on his overstressed blood pump. He had a lot of police company during his stay. A police officer in his hospital room noted, "DICICCO in bed, woke up when we arrived. Advised us he is going to need a heart bypass — DICICCO into shower." Later, another officer noted, "Male in room 4716 — Male sleeping — Male awake, turns T.V. on — Asleep again," etc. Still another officer in DiCicco's room noted, "Male calls lawyer. Randall BARR's office calls. Male speaks on phone. Male off phone, informing [officer that] . . . lawyer can't make bail hearing tomorrow (weather). Unknown if lawyer is going to call courts. Male asking for assistance, maybe call his lawyer, 416-366-6466. Call made [to] lawyer. Speaks with . . . BARR, informs he has called crown and . . . advice made."

On one occasion, a police officer urged DiCicco to become an informer. From his hospital bed, through the confusion and exhaustion and pain flowing through his mind, DiCicco replied, "You're either in or you're out. I will take my chances." What about going into the witness protection program? "No way," DiCicco scoffed. "Those guys will find you anywhere. I'll take my chances. I know I'm going to jail, it's just a matter of how long."

· · · · · · ·

Police set up a few trailers on-site as command centers, and police vans and cars were scattered across the property. Over the next few days, heavy snowstorms, slippery roads, extreme wind and extreme cold complicated the police operation.

Some officers investigated. Some, like Bednarcyzk, selected, packed away, organized and documented the evidence. Some secured the scene. Others followed up on clues. Some were managers. Some dealt with the media. Some handled logistics. Some helped to destroy contraband. Others drove to pick up bottled water or Tim Hortons coffee or food from Swiss Chalet, Pizza Hut and Licks Burgers, to hydrate and feed the many police officers working overtime on the case. Some of the officers were assigned to dealing with the hundreds of emailed Crime Stopper tips police were receiving and at least one phoned-in false confession, as well as nervous calls from the building's insurer, asking about structural damage, mold and other risks associated with grow ops. One officer cleared snow off the command-center trailer roof. Another dealt with the problem of plastic Porta Potties whose contents had frozen solid in the ridiculously cold weather. One officer was sent out to deal with an apparent trespasser on the Molson property; it turned out to be a reporter from the *Globe and Mail*.

． ． ． ． ． ．

After the identification team had combed through the entire place, photographing and videorecording — with long-haired Bednarcyzk starring in several of the videos, guiding the cameraman through the labyrinth of evidence — it was time to dismantle and collect the evidence in a way that would hold up in court.

Bednarcyzk was in charge of the dismantling team. Nicknamed "Bedrock," he'd been doing this kind of work for three years. Like Bleich, who was around the same age and also liked to eat at Kelsey's, he was good at logistics. Supervising the dismantling while making his own investigations, Bednarcyzk was on-site for two weeks, 12 to 15 hours a day.

His team counted plants and weighed bags of flowers: there were 10,272 plants on the Ontario Pallet side and 9,865 on the Barrie Good Fish side. Total: 20,137 plants and 169 pounds of dried flowers, not including plants and flowers found at the two minor grow ops at Molson or the 3,000 babies discovered at Oro.

The officers cut down all the now-wilting plants and stuffed them into garbage bags. They took all of the HID bulbs out of the dangling reflectors and disconnected the heating and air-conditioning systems. Bednarcyzk later said, "The electrical system was beyond my scope, so I called Mr. Wyers [a local electrical contractor] to disconnect."

John Wyers, assisted by his brother Christian, inspected the wires and told the police that "the wiring was unsafe . . . A 600 volt electrical panel open to the environment . . . There is no support for the wires, they are just strung everywhere . . . This new wire installation is not to code and not done properly . . . If it were a legitimate business, the hydro inspector [would] never [have] allowed the ballasts in that condition . . . None of this installed electrical work is up to building code and would not be allowed."

On the roof, the Wyers brothers found and removed the massive wire that, years ago, Bleich, DaSilva, McGee and the tradesmen from Quebec, all high on cocaine, had struggled with.

A waste disposal service was hired to remove and, with the help of the City of Barrie, dispose of thousands of gallons of farm chemicals, mainly fertilizers — even though at least two Barrie police officers had said the chemicals were "essentially safe."

Some of the police work involved going into dangerous situations — there was always the risk of running into desperate gardeners. One officer wrote in his notebook, "Due to magnitude of grow, we should assume that they may be armed to defend it." There were rumors of a secret tunnel, where the gardeners were waiting for the police to leave. "Keep eye for hidden walls + secret doors," another officer noted.

To find any concealed gardeners, police used a flexible camera that could poke through walls and twist around corners, as well as night-vision goggles and a FLIR thermovision body-heat sensor.

Other dangers included fires, electric shocks and trip hazards, which were rife in the complex. Officers wore harnesses when they were working at heights. There was a gas leak one night, which could

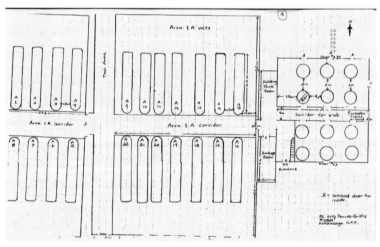

Police sketch by Kelly Daniels-Griffis [Ontario Provincial Police]

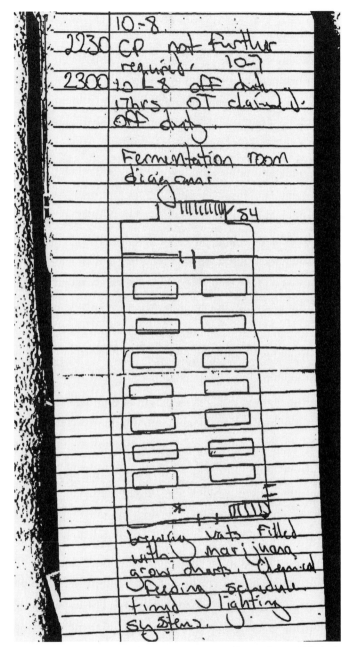

Police sketch from Constable S. Anthony's notebook [Ontario Provincial Police]

have led to a major explosion; Enbridge workers came to fix the breached gas line.

In confined places, such as growing tanks, officers wore machines that measured air quality and made sure that firefighters were close by. Some rooms were unsafe because of acids used as floor cleansers. At least one OPP officer worried about uncovering a toxic methamphetamine lab.

One officer noted, "LIVE ELECTRICITY! . . . SYRINGES!"

. . . .

Some areas in the building were heated, some were freezing cold. Some had working lights, while others were dark. But all had to be searched and secured, with police officers occasionally shouting, "Police! Search warrant!"

"Offence related property" from the Molson building — such as tools, equipment, etc. — filled more than two large metal bins. The officers seized 701 HID bulbs, 698 shades, 704 ballasts, 18 water pumps, 77 fans, 39 charcoal filter units and 26 air-conditioning units. They also seized many personal items from the bedrooms and kitchens, things that carried fingerprints. These would be sent to the RCMP for analysis.

Samples of the seized flowers were sent to federal laboratories to be tested by chemists and determined to be cannabis. Some flowers went to the RCMP for DNA analysis.

Barrie Police Chief Wayne Frechette was asked by a *Barrie Examiner* journalist what would happen to the rest of the seized cannabis. He said that "burning it would take ages," adding that many people had expressed a desire to be downwind of the bud bonfire.

Authorized by an "emergency destruction order," the remaining flowers and 20,137 dead plants were taken in several dumptrucks to the Barrie dump. A civilian bulldozer operator buried the contraband in a 10-foot-deep hole and covered it with garbage. According to Tracy McLaughlin of the *Sun*, a few years earlier police had seized

30,000 cannabis plants from an outdoor farm just north of Barrie. These plants and flowers had been buried in a dump in nearby Orillia. That night, people had snuck onto the dump with shovels to dig up the plants. For months after that, people in Orillia had smoked the back-from-the-grave "dump weed."

That did not happen this time. Armed police officers guarded the buried salad until it rotted.

Briefing

The #1 piece of advice from criminal defense lawyers:
"IF ARRESTED, DO NOT TALK AT ALL TO POLICE. SAY NOTHING."

Darkness at Noon

"You'll be in Joyceville or Millhaven. Start at the maximum securities, 'cause everyone starts there. So you'll start with all the bad boys . . . You got caught with your hand in the cookie jar."
— Officer Rusty Watson

January 11. The afternoon after the raid.

One of the arrested gardeners was 23-year-old Scott Dillon. He stood five-seven and weighed about 150 pounds. He had brown hair and green eyes, and a scar on the left side of his nose. He lived with his parents in Etobicoke, a suburb of Toronto.

Dillon was interviewed by Officer Rusty Watson at the Barrie police station. These are excerpts from his time in the interview room:

Officer Rusty Watson: . . . Okay, um, hmm. What else can we shoot the shit about? So, if you had any job in the world, what would you want?

Scott Dillon: I guess I wish I stayed in school and would become a biomedical analyst.

Watson: What the hell is a biomedical analyst?

Dillon: It's computers and biology and find a cure for cancer and that stuff like that . . .

Watson: Why didn't you stay in school? What happened there?

Dillon: I got too old.

Watson: You got too old? Oh, you were having too much fun in high school and they wouldn't let you stick around no more?

Dillon: Yeah, pretty much.

Watson: . . . So the last four or five years of high school were a pretty good party?

Dillon: Pretty much all of high school.

Watson: . . . Do you go to the casino a lot?

Dillon: No.

Watson: Did you ever play?

Dillon: No, I don't gamble.

Watson: You don't gamble. You're taking a really big gamble now.

Dillon: I'm taking a very big gamble.

Watson: You're taking a big gamble. What's the worst can happen to you in this, do you think?

Dillon: I get five years, six years.

Watson: Five, six years, yeah. You think that'd be — Have you ever been to jail? . . .

Dillon: It's not easy to stomach, but —

Watson: But five to six years — Where — what do you think you'll end up at?

Dillon: I don't know . . .

Watson: You'll be in Joyceville or Millhaven. Start at the maximum securities, 'cause everyone starts there. So you'll start with all the bad boys . . . You got caught with your hand in the cookie jar. You know, you got caught with something big. That's a whole lot of millions of dollars. People who owned it aren't going to be happy it's gone. You know. The public will be really happy. The public will be great. The public will be happy that this bad dope is taken off the street. You know.

Dillon: Who's dying? How bad is it? Who's dying? I see people die every day.

Watson: I know: there's coke and heroin; there's ecstasy . . .

Dillon: I see things differently.

Watson: You know, I agree. It's all public perception. I agree there is a lot worse dope out there than weed. Okay. I agree . . . Okay, I believe that. That's true.

Dillon: Yeah. But look at cigarettes. Cigarettes serves as just as much of a gateway as dope is . . . [Tobacco is] legal 'cause the government gets rid of it. But all it really is is a package for the government to get rid of their drug.

Watson: The packages make money. Their taxes. Booze.

Dillon: And booze, and the same thing with weed. It will be legalized one day . . .

Watson: I mean, we could argue what's good, what's bad all day long. There's guys that sit there — and you talk to Rastafarians from Jamaica — they would say, "Bob Marley's great." He died of cancer.

Dillon: Yeah.

Watson: You know, these guys are saying that one set of rules, that's the way they want to live their life — that's fine by me. If you want to be Jewish and not eat pork, hey, fine by me. You want to be Amish and drive a horse and buggy, hey, that's your life. You made choices. I'm not going to impose my values on you and I don't expect you to do the same for me . . . If you got anything, anything you want to get off your chest. You know, it could be about anything. It could be about how you think that Bob Marley was framed by the guy who shot JFK. Whatever you want. Nothing you can think of? Just trying to figure out how you are going to get yourself out of this mess you got yourself in?

Dillon: That's about it.

Watson: Yeah? Big mess?

Dillon: It's a fuck of a mess . . .

. . . .

Another of the arrested gardeners, Craig Walker, was the brother of the manager of the Ontario Pallet grow rooms, Scott Walker. Craig lived in Niagara Falls. He was just over six feet tall and weighed 218 pounds. He had brown eyes, and tattoos of a dragon, a cross and a skull. He had worked for 11 years for Redpath Sugar in Niagara Falls as a manager in a shipping warehouse and had quit just a few months earlier, because after a change in management, he said, he "butted heads with management too much, I couldn't take it." He had two sons, 12 and 13 years old, and was paying their mother $1,000 in child support every month. "I was making good money," he said.

From Craig Walker's time in the interview room with Officer P. Kellachan at the Barrie police station:

Officer P. Kellachan: . . . You haven't been in trouble before. You haven't gone through this system before. All right. If you have a question or problem, you understand, we're here, we can help you out too just as much as they can. We basically investigate. We're not out here — we don't come up here and show up and say, "You know what? Craig Walker, you know, that asshole, we're going to arrest him tonight." That's not how it works.

Craig Walker: That's what happened. I had *20* guys pointing guns at my head. One guy grabbed my nuts and squeezed my nuts. Hurting me in the nuts.

Kellachan: Well, there is an ongoing investigation.

Walker: I have my rights, you know.

Kellachan: So, I'm not saying that gives anybody the right —

Walker: You don't physically abuse people.

. . . .

Rayne Sauve, another of the arrested gardeners, was part Native Canadian. When arrested, he had crack cocaine hidden in his underwear. He was 36 and lived in St. Catharines. He was allergic to penicillin, had lost his driver's license because of unpaid fines and had a criminal record for failure to appear in court, impaired driving, possession of stolen property, drug possession and break and enter. He was covered with various tattoos he'd had inked when he was 16, including one of his name on his arm. He had kids but did not live with their mother.

In the interview room at the Barrie police station, Sauve complained to Officer S. Connor about another man who was in custody:

Rayne Sauve: Get rid of that guy if you can. He's a fucking loudmouth.
Officer S. Connor: What's that?
Sauve: If you could give him a sleeping pill or something.
Connor: Which one?
Sauve:The guy in the fucking — in the tank there. Keeps banging on the walls.
Connor: Is he a drunk or — ?
Sauve: I don't know. He's a loser, though . . . he didn't want to wait for a lineup in Walmart. So he just walked out with the stuff.
Connor: Went postal?
Sauve: Yeah. [Both laugh] . . .

At the end of the video recording, Sauve yelled, "Where's my pizza and beer?!"

. . . .

Zoran Stajanovik was another gardener caught in the raid. He had been born in Bosnia, had come to Canada in 1989 and was now a Canadian citizen. On arrival in Canada, he had lived in Elliot Lake, working in a mine, and then he moved to Thompson, Manitoba, and later to Ottawa, then Toronto and finally St. Catharines. He stood about five-three, weighed about 150 pounds and had a damaged finger on his left hand. He had a daughter, who lived in St. Catharines, and was separated from his wife, who lived in Toronto. He was a self-employed mechanic, repairing vehicles in the parking lot of his apartment building. He said his education had been "a little bit of high school."

At one point during his interrogation by police officers, he said, "I don't know what to say. I don't know what to say. I don't know why you stop me. I don't have weapons. I don't know dope. I don't know nothing. I never use this in my life. I know this — one day you will see!"

. . . .

From Officer Brent Bergeron's interview with Scott Walker, the manager of the Ontario Pallet part of the grow op who'd missed the warning because he'd let his phone batteries go dead:

Officer Brent Bergeron: As you probably put two and two together, uh, you probably know why you are here. We found a large amount of marijuana growing at Molson Centre and, um, you guys have all been — you know why you're charged.
Scott Walker: They say I'm charged with cultivation . . .
Bergeron: Exactly. Um, where were you born and raised? In St. Catharines? Okay. And are those the guys that you were riding with last night, are those friends of yours?
Walker: I just picked them up. I don't know.
Bergeron: Had you met them before?
Walker: No. I want a lawyer. I've been asking for a lawyer since I got booked. They will not give me a lawyer.
Bergeron: Have you spoken to one?
Walker: No, I spoke to some duty counselor in Toronto last

night and he fed me a line of shit. I don't even know if it was a lawyer.

Bergeron: Right.

Walker: I want a lawyer. And I've been asking for a lawyer for the last *24* hours and I want a lawyer. And there, I don't get to make a phone call, nothing. I want a lawyer. We're all asking for lawyers.

Bergeron: Okay.

Walker: We have that right, don't we?

Bergeron: Sure. Well, you have the right to speak to a lawyer, like you did last night.

Walker: Yeah?

Bergeron: I think that, um, I'm not sure. I know that you guys will be going before a justice of the peace for your bail hearing.

Walker: Uh-huh.

Bergeron: And that will probably be Monday, I believe.

Walker: Well, see, they bullshit us. They told us it was this morning [Saturday] . . . The lawyer told me last night that I would have a bail hearing today, no matter what. That's my right. Within *24* hours of being detained, I'm allowed to have a bail hearing. And what happened? Where is it?

Bergeron: But that's not right.

Walker: See, then he was feeding me a line of shit then. You know what I mean. So, obviously, he wasn't a lawyer . . .

. . . . . .

Michael DiCicco — suffering from his diabetes and heart problems — was brought to the interview room of the Barrie police station, where he spoke with Officer Rusty Watson.

Officer Rusty Watson: Do you live with anyone now? You live by yourself.

Michael DiCicco: My cat.

Watson: Your cat. What type of cat do you have?

DiCicco: A black cat. I don't know what kind he is.

Watson: Like a pound cat or a pet store?

DiCicco: Yeah. A tomcat.

Watson: What's his name?

DiCicco: Bubbas . . . I think they took him away. I don't know. I'm worried about him.

Watson: Okay. Well, we don't usually go around arresting cats. So —

DiCicco: Yeah, but you can't leave him alone.

Watson: Does he got a litter box? He's got food out? Cats are a lot better than dogs. You can't leave dogs alone. Dogs would tear your house apart . . . How long have you had the cat?

DiCicco: Five, six years.

Watson: Good company?

DiCicco: Yeah.

Watson: Yeah? What do you do for recreation? Do you water-ski, mountain climb, skydive, parasail?

DiCicco: I got a bad heart. I can't do anything.

Watson: . . . So, you're not married. Single with a cat. You got any kids?

DiCicco: I got four kids.

Watson: Four kids. You're a braver man than me.

DiCicco: [laughs] I had five.

Watson: Oh, I'm sorry to hear that. What happened?

DiCicco: One died.

Watson: A daughter?

DiCicco: A son . . .

Watson: Yeah, so are you a granddad yet?

DiCicco: Yeah. I have *13* of them.

Watson: . . . Why not talk to the police?

DiCicco: . . . I can't answer any of your questions. I'm sorry. You're tricking me or trying to trick me. I can't do that. I need my lawyer. I'm sorry.

On Tuesday, January 20 — 10 days after the raid — a Barrie Police officer found Bubbas the cat, still alive inside the old beer store.

. . . .

From Officer Rusty Watson's interview with Robert Bleich, the St. Catharines-based Ozzy Osbourne fan who'd built the Ontario Pallet side with Jeff "The Frenchman" DaSilva:

Robert Bleich: [My fiancée] is eight and a half months pregnant right now.
Officer Rusty Watson: First?
Bleich: Yeah. And this is not going to go over too well.
Watson: No, I can imagine this is going to stress her life now.
Bleich: Oh, she [will be] pretty bitchy. [laughs]
Watson: I've been there, you know, I've been there with the wife and kids. I know exactly what it's like.
Bleich: It's our first, so, you know.
Watson: The first. Your first fiancée too?
Bleich: Yeah, everything.
Watson: Boy, you're like, uh —
Bleich: Yeah, I got myself between a rock and a hard place now.
Watson: Okay, well, I'm just more interested in talking about the fiancée right now.
Bleich: Yeah.
Watson: So, how long have you known her?
Bleich: Seven years.
Watson: Seven years. Is she from St. Catharines too?
Bleich: Uh-huh.
Watson: Yeah, and you lived in St. Catharines your whole life?
. . . Now, St. Catharines has a . . . big bridge that goes over the seaway — is it the canal? Where the boats go?

Bleich: Uh-huh.

Watson: Okay. Whereabouts — how close to that do you live?

. . .

Bleich: Right around there.

Watson: Right around there. Okay . . . Now, what do you do? Do you work? Um, are you a plumber, electrician, a firefighter, fighter pilot?

Bleich: Self-employed.

Watson: Self-employed? What kind of stuff?

Bleich: Construction. Just contracts. Cash stuff.

Watson: Right on. You know, you gotta make a living somehow.

Bleich: Yep.

Watson: . . . Who was in the van with you?

Bleich: I don't know . . .

Watson: We stopped you for a reason. You know what that reason is?

Bleich: No.

Watson: No? Just —

Bleich: Well, I found out now. Yeah.

Watson: You found out? What did you find out?

Bleich: Some little P.P., whatever that means. Purpose —

Watson: Possession for the purpose of trafficking.

Bleich: And something else.

Watson: Cultivation?

Bleich: I don't know if it was conspiracy or something?

Watson: Conspiracy would be like if you shot JFK.

Bleich: [laughs] They said there was a couple of things.

Watson: No. Uh, possession for the purpose of trafficking marijuana, which basically means there is more marijuana than Bob Marley could smoke in a year. You could probably get away with possession for him, but in a normal guy like you and me, it's a whole lot more than most of us smoke in a lifetime.

Bleich: Uh-huh . . .

Watson: You know your vehicle was stopped. Um, I was just curious what your day entailed. Where did you start? Like, where were you off to? When you were stopped, where were you going?

Bleich: Uh-huh.

Watson: Nowhere? You were just driving around?

Bleich: Just driving around.

Watson: Just driving around. And the guys you were with?

Bleich: No clue.

Watson: No clue. Where'd you pick them up at? Or how'd they get in? They just magically appear in your van?

Bleich: Uh-huh.

Later, Bleich said, "If I'm gone for five years, I'm gone for five years and I don't care. Whatever happens, happens."

Briefing

In 2003, across all of Ontario, police seized 232,000 cannabis plants.

In both Quebec and British Columbia that year, police seized much larger amounts.

On December 2, 2004, police in Manitoba raided a Winnipeg warehouse just a few blocks away from police headquarters. Inside, officers found Canada's second-biggest grow op: 10,000 cannabis plants, with a police-estimated value of $11 million.

Many more raids would follow. Year after year after year, raid after raid after raid. To cannabis farmers and dealers, raids were a cost of doing business, added to the price paid by the end consumer. When one criminal group was jailed, another took its place.

Raids barely, if at all, affect supply.

The Morning
after a Party

*"There were these huge steel doors that must have blocked off
the marijuana from us, but everybody talked about it. All day long
you would see these strange people walking in and out . . . The
way the plant was put together, it was the perfect place for a
marijuana operation. The rumors were rampant that it was a
massive marijuana factory."*
— Anonymous source

Dismantling the Barrie grow op was dangerous, especially when police officers shut off the heat to the building, causing water pipes to freeze and burst, spraying water over live electrical wires. Twenty firefighters were kept on standby. There would be many more burst pipes and leaks to come — all fixed by reluctant handyman Larry McGee.

McGee had to do maintenance on the boilers twice every day. Escorted at all times by a pair of Barrie Police officers, he kept the boilers going and set up some propane space heaters to prevent more pipes from freezing. McGee also helped the police with other mechanical tasks, like fixing a broken door. Soon, he would demand a vacation, training his own replacement.

McGee went to the police station six times to be interviewed. Bob DeRosa was suspicious that he was helping the police. In the end, despite the hydroponic grow room found attached to his bedroom, McGee was not charged with anything. They let him go.

· · · · · ·

Canadian and international news outlets ran stories about the Barrie raid. One evocatively described "a tropical jungle of marijuana plants stretching into the distance of the vast building." Another quoted an officer saying that the plants "went on and on," comparing the sight to "a little Saskatchewan."

A *Toronto Star* article written by Betsy Powell and Roberta Avery quoted an OPP superintendent who claimed, "There's everything from seed —" incorrect — no seeds were found "— to packaged plants for distribution. I suspect we'll be in there for weeks gathering evidence and our forensic people will be in there for several weeks more dismantling it. There's miles and miles and miles of electrical wire and water hoses. It's incredible."

Powell and Avery added:

> A former tenant who ran a business from the complex said another of the companies would continually roast coffee beans, which would also mask any smell.
>
> The tenant said internal loading docks — there are external docks as well — would allow the possibility of shipping out products undercover.
>
> And even though the site is visible to thousands of daily commuters, it also provided adequate camouflage, say authorities.
>
> The windowless building has parkland on the east and north sides, Highway 400 to the west and trees to the south, so it is not overlooked by other businesses apart from a seasonal garden centre, which is presently closed. . . .
>
> [Another] former tenant didn't suspect anything, but in

hindsight now realizes there were obvious signs.

Aside from the people living at the plant — "I figured they had nowhere else to go" — the former tenant now suspects the need for 24-hour security, the boiler blowing up one day and constant mechanical upgrades for a paucity of products being shipped from the site.

"There were tonnes of skids of coffee beans.

"That and marble tile," said the tenant.

"I never saw anything go out the door. I saw it coming in."

An inspector for the City of Barrie's water department told police about meeting Bob DeRosa, whom he described as a "big, tall, deaf guy." The inspector added, "There was also rumors about pot being grown there and the rumor was that there were mob connections. It was just rumors that everybody talked about."

A cleaning woman at the Molson building told police, "What caught my attention was there would be this straight truck, a burgundy one that would come by every once in a while and drop off, say, one or two washer-dryers or things like that, still in the boxes. I thought for sure that it was stolen property just because there would be only one or two items. Then the guys who unloaded were biker types, you know. Harley shirts, beards, long hair, that kind of thing. They'd bring in their bikes and wash them too. They were nice to us. Now I know about the bikers from my hubby because he looks like one. I recognized an Outlaws tattoo on one guy because he used the washroom. That's basically why I thought it was all shady. I mean, I never heard anything about grows or pot, so I can't say anything about that."

A manager of the car-parts company in the building at first did not want to talk to police, saying she was "nervous and upset" because she had seen Para-Dice Riders bikers hanging around the property. Later, when she calmed down, she told police, "I joked with [a National Roasters employee] that there was more going on up there than just coffee. Just because of all the people . . . I was of the opinion that there was drugs happening. [The National Roasters employee] would just laugh at me."

A man who had worked on the site for a film company anonymously told the *Sun*, "You just knew that someone was producing pot in there. There were these huge steel doors that must have blocked off the marijuana from us, but everybody talked about it. All day long you would see these strange people walking in and out . . . The way the plant was put together, it was the perfect place for a marijuana operation. The rumors were rampant that it was a massive marijuana factory."

Many of the people working for companies at the Molson building recalled drinking beer in Larry McGee's apartment. None, however, recalled seeing the hydroponic jungle attached to McGee's bedroom.

An employee at the Barrie Home Depot, questioned by police, remembered serving Robert Bleich. She said he would pay with $100 bills, spending thousands of dollars at a time. She would check the bills to make sure they were not counterfeit. Sometimes she'd joke with Bleich, saying things like, "You guys must be selling dope over there to have the cash you have."

A sales clerk at Plant Products in Brampton later recognized Bleich in a newspaper photo. She described him to police as "very friendly . . . tall, six-one to six-two, brown hair parted to one side. He's thinner, might be fit, but always wore a sweater . . . definitely a familiar face." She had dreaded seeing him take out his wallet, as it was a big hassle to count the large amount of paper money he'd always use to pay — $2,000 to $5,000 each time.

Another female sales clerk at Plant Products remembered Bleich as "a very polite and friendly customer . . . tall, nice-sized frame to him, six feet or a little more. Light-colored hair. Well-kept. Looked nice, clean."

Another recalled to police, "He is a very friendly fellow and always chats with us when he comes in . . . He always seemed so nice . . . We all knew him."

A message to the media [Mark O'Neill]

When Bleich was released on bail, he got annoyed at the journalists crowding around him and his eight-and-a-half-month-pregnant fiancée as they walked in the corridors of the Newmarket courthouse. As Bleich stepped out of the courthouse building at 4:00 a.m., he smiled and raised a middle finger to a *Toronto Sun* photographer; the *Sun* published the picture, making Bleich famous.

A while later, while his case was still working its way through the system, Bleich went to a Yuk Yuk's comedy club. He learned that one of his heroes, Tommy Chong — of the comedy duo Cheech and Chong — was also in the club. Bleich went over to the gray-haired celebrity and introduced himself. When he mentioned that he had been recently arrested for cannabis cultivation, and that he had been pictured in the *Toronto Sun* giving the finger to the world, Chong said something like, "I saw that! Man, you are my hero!" Chong made a big deal about Bleich's accomplishments and proudly introduced Bleich to his wife, who was also a big fan of Robert Bleich's work.

· · · · · · ·

Police had a lot of success collecting information about Diccico. Approached by officers, fish farmer Dave Atlantis — who had run Barrie Good Fish with Diccico until contamination killed the tiny tilapia — initially answered their questions, then he became upset, yelling, "I don't know and I can't remember all this shit . . . I am going to get a lawyer and I am going to watch what I fucking say because I don't want to get shot tomorrow. I have a wife and a child."

An officer asked him to calm down.

Asked why anyone would want to shoot him, Atlantis said, "If it was a $100 million operation — What the fuck, I don't want to say dick . . . I know nothing, I don't give a crap, because I had nothing to do with it."

"Calm down and relax," an officer said.

Atlantis managed to settle down and proceeded to answer more questions about Mike DiCicco and Barrie Good Fish.

It wasn't long after the police interview that Atlantis developed a growth in his brain that caused him many serious health problems, including massive loss of memory. Within a few years, he would not be able to remember anything about the period of his life in the Molson building.

· · · · · · ·

Some of the success of the investigation was due to good police work; some to luck.

For example, DiCicco's ex-wife saw, during TV news coverage of the Molson raid, that some of the furniture used in the grow op belonged to her. According to a police officer's notes, she "got pissed and dropped a dime [i.e., phoned the police with information]."

. . . .

The raid was a big topic of conversation in Ontario and elsewhere. Many people decided to pipe in with their opinions.

The mayor of Barrie, Rob Hamilton, said, "Even the bad guys understand Barrie is a tremendous place to do business."

Barrie Police Chief Wayne Frechette weighed in too: "It's not the distinction that the city of Barrie was hoping for."

Soon after the raid, Nancy Tuckett, Barrie's director of economic development, said, "There's no residential development anywhere to take issue with odors or anything. There's no one around really in the vicinity other than the plant itself, so yes, it sounds surprising, but the truth be known, there's nothing within several hundred [yards] of the plant."

The president of Barrie Hydro said there was only one electric meter for the entire building and that the amount of electricity used was much less than when Molson had been making beer, adding, "There was nothing unusual to alert anyone to what was going on in there."

Several newspapers quoted a deputy commissioner of the OPP, who called the Barrie grow op "the largest and most sophisticated in Canada," and Police Chief Frechette, who said, "I am very pleased that we were able to shut down and dismantle what was the largest indoor marijuana growing operation within Canada; the fact that it resided in our community demonstrates the need for the public to be vigilant for suspicious activities which may be evidence of illegal drug production."

Police urged people to read the OPP *Green Tide* report (available online as a free download), which described the "significant societal threats" posed by grow ops in Ontario.

A spokesperson for the Molson brewing corporation told a reporter, "We sold the place three years ago. We have no comment."

Vincent DeRosa did not return repeated calls from reporters. He issued a statement through defense lawyer John Wolf, denying involvement and calling himself a "victim."

Fercan's finance director told a reporter, "Those things have nothing to do with the matters at hand and I have nothing further to say."

Gordon Laschinger — a Conservative Party activist and ethanol promoter who had worked closely with Vincent DeRosa on real estate and ethanol deals over many years — described Fercan as falling into a trap that awaits landlords who "rent out industrial properties to tenants on a net-rent basis where the tenants basically look after the premises. The risk is, if you don't inspect regularly, you can find that these operations can spring up." Laschinger told the *Globe and Mail* that Fercan was "scrambling" to inspect its other properties, to avoid more surprises.

Fercan general manager Italo Ferrari told the *Hamilton Spectator*, "We cannot always get up there to check. We have properties all over southern Ontario." To the *Toronto Star*, Ferrari said, "We don't know who comes and who goes."

Asked about Vincent DeRosa, an OPP officer said, "He owns both spots and there's marijuana growing at both spots. We'll definitely be looking into that coincidence." OPP Detective Rick Barnum said the Fercan ownership of the buildings was "definitely curious . . . It is the next logical step to investigate that connection and look into it further."

"Most people find it amusing," defense lawyer Randall Barrs told reporters. "It shows that the public does not see marijuana as a social problem. On the other hand, if you look at what was produced in the plant before . . . It is kind of ironic because society does perceive alcohol as a huge problem . . . It is the criminalization of marijuana that has caused a criminal element and organized crime — just like [alcohol] Prohibition." He pointed out that alcohol and cigarettes cause much more harm to society.

To a judge hearing the case, Barrs said, "If the government was successful in stamping out grow houses in Canada . . . we'd be back to importing marijuana from Mexico and South America . . . The fact is that for many, many Canadians — from British Columbia to ski country in the Barrie area — these guys are almost like local heroes, that's the irony. If you read the press on this that came out at the onset, this whole episode was the subject of a great deal of amusement and the subject of a lot of jokes both by Canadian and American entertainers."

One such entertainer was U.S. singer and actor Bette Midler. In a 2004 New York radio interview, discussing the grow op at the beer factory, Midler called Barrie "your one-spot stop-and-shop for booze and pot!"

For years afterwards, every January 9, a Barrie radio station commemorated the anniversary of the raid on the Molson grow op, treating it like a significant historical event.

Which, maybe, it was.

. . . .

Three of the men arrested had their charges dropped. The other six pled guilty. When invited by the judge to make a statement before sentencing, every one of them said, "No comment." Depending on their criminal records, the growers were sentenced to prison terms ranging from two to five years.

Michael "the Old Guy" DiCicco appeared confused in the courtroom. His health condition — he had heart disease, diabetes, bad legs, partial deafness, partial blindness and an amputated left big toe — led the judge to say, "A jail term may well prove fatal." So DiCicco got to serve his two-year sentence "in the community," not behind bars. Despite his illness, DiCicco was strong enough to shove a journalist outside the courtroom.

Robert Bleich got five years. His wife gave birth just before his sentencing. Their daughter would later be found to have a genius-level IQ.

While in prison, Bleich continued trafficking. At Beaver Creek — a minimum-security prison near Gravenhurst, Ontario — he arranged for someone to leave a quarter pound of cannabis on the grounds of the Gravenhurst airport. An inmate on a work detail near there picked up the package and brought it to Bleich in prison. Bleich hid the weed — worth much more in the prison marketplace than outside the walls — in a freezer, where a guard found it. They could not prove it belonged to Bleich but, suspicious, they transferred him to a medium-security prison.

· · · · · · ·

A December 4, 2004, *Globe and Mail* article noted, "While the sentences put the farmers in jail, the police still have not arrested those who benefited the most from the operation, which, police estimated, produced marijuana with a value between $8.6-million and $60-million a year."

Police told the *Toronto Star* that the sentenced men were minor players. Regarding the publicly unidentified and at-large masterminds, OPP Superintendent Jim Miller said, "We know who's behind it. But we've got to have evidence to prove it in court and we just don't have it . . . I would have loved to have been able to step back and watch the comings and goings [at the Molson building] for six months."

Later, the *Globe* reported that Vincent DeRosa's Fercan corporation owed the City of Barrie $648,000 in taxes on the Molson property, having paid no property taxes at all in 2003. The same article noted that Fercan — which owned the Eaton Centre in downtown Hamilton — also owed $101,000 in Hamilton taxes.

Fercan had further been accused by Hamilton resident Joanna

Chapman of breaking the Municipal Election Act, for allegedly making an illegal campaign donation (a rent-free campaign office in the Eaton Center) to the re-election campaign of Hamilton mayor Larry DiIanni, who was convicted of breaking election-finance laws; charges against Fercan were not pursued.

The Barrie investigation — called "Project Plants" — had, within a few months, cost Ontario taxpayers over $500,000 in expenses and police time.

The investigation would eventually change its name to "Project 3D" and then "Project Birmingham" and continue, seeking the Molson plant "masterminds."

. . . .

After the raids, the gang splintered.

Glenn Day did not see Jeff DaSilva around for a long time.

Fred Freeman turned off his phone and went to B.C. for a few months, where he started dealing Ritalin. A then-fashionable synthetic chemical designed to treat attention deficit disorder, Ritalin was sometimes used in the belief that it would give one an intellectual advantage over one's rivals (during a math exam, for example). When Freeman returned to Ontario, he stayed away from Drago Dolic's meetings at the massage parlour and their association fizzled out.

Dolic did not seem much affected by the raids. He switched his focus to cocaine deals with Hop Sing, the drug dealer who'd socialized with Dolic's gang at the massage parlour and expensive Toronto-area restaurants. He also hired a retired couple from Quebec, Serge and Diana Bernier, who used their trailer camper to courier Dolic's cocaine, cannabis and money around North America. He believed he could trust them.

Davorka Pelikan, meanwhile, stayed away from her drug-industry contacts and burned the written records of her clippers. Once, watching a TV news piece about the Barrie grow op, she saw video footage of her purple-walled room and her leopard-print bedsheets. She missed the money and excitement of clipping.

After the police raid, the other businesses renting space at the Molson building gradually moved out. There was talk of converting the place to an ethanol-production facility. Much of the old Molson equipment, including the tanks, was scavenged and sold.

National Roasters stopped operating. The company left behind in the building about 56,000 pounds of green coffee beans in 130- and 2,000-pound bags, perhaps worth over $150,000.

Eventually, except for Aurora Beverage, which still did some water-bottling business, the property was abandoned. The crumbling, rainwater-damaged, junk-strewn, police-vandalized structure, however, was still looked after by Fercan maintenance man Larry McGee.

Years after the raid, a trespasser in the empty building would report, on his blog, that parts of the old building still smelled like cannabis, while other parts still reeked of coffee.

. . . .

Shortly after the raid, Bob DeRosa was fired by Fercan. Despite that, he was able to give his assistant/driver, Hazel Lane, a $50,000 bonus. She used it to buy some farmland and start raising cattle.

DeRosa started a corporation, R.J.C. Construction, which sometimes earned contracts to do work — like demolishing an old psychiatric hospital in Whitby, Ontario — for one of his younger brother's corporations.

In 2005, DeRosa arranged financing, using false documents, for Lane to buy a house at 17 Guest Road, in Oro. It was his idea, not hers.

One of DeRosa's friends, a trucker who had worked for National Roasters, moved into the house and, for about three years, paid rent to Lane. When he moved out and the rent checks stopped, Lane was forced into bankruptcy. She lost both 17 Guest Road and her home, the cattle farm. A year after the trucker left — April 27, 2009 — an

OPP raid at 17 Guest Road found a cannabis grow op, including 4,000 babies. Nobody was charged.

. . . .

Winter, 2008.

Half of the famous Molson brewery — constructed by Benson & Hedges in 1970 — was torn down by ProGreen Demolition, for a fee of $2.2 million. ProGreen estimated that 98 percent of the material from the building would be recycled.

Bit by bit, machines with robot arms smashed apart and dragged away the Molson building. Metal claws tore the walls into chunks. Other machines used chains to drag out the big stainless-steel tanks that had once created a lot of beer, then a lot of cannabis, then a lot of police overtime.

The tanks were to be sold, the demolition company's president explained to the media — "that means you can't scratch or damage them." The price of stainless steel was rising and the tanks would eventually bring in $3 million for Fercan. ProGreen was the same demolition company that had once dismantled the Molson factory in downtown Toronto, just off Lakeshore Boulevard, where, many years earlier, Drago Dolic had set up one of his very first grow ops.

BOOK II

Briefing

Brownsville, Texas, is just across the border from Mexico.

By 2005, the previous main south-to-north cocaine smuggling route —
through the Caribbean and Florida, as depicted in the TV show Miami
Vice — had fallen out of favor. Since then, 90 percent of the cocaine
entering the U.S. has come through Mexico. Most of the cocaine entering
Canada comes from the U.S.

When cocaine — chemically, an alkaline salt — is put on the tongue, it
tastes bitter and increases saliva flow. Part of the tongue feels numb, then
frosty.

Cocaine users like this feeling and want more.

Brain scans indicate that the craving that cocaine users feel for cocaine is
similar to the craving that salt eaters feel for salt.

 Dolic's Doom

"Huge amounts of costs by your government and ours, lawyers all over the place, all so a bunch of nuts in Toronto could have a little cocaine and destroy their lives."
— Texas Judge Lynn Hughes

In 2005, Drago Dolic was in Canada, talking on the telephone with an American cocaine dealer named Thoi Uc Do. Dolic was doing a lot of business with people of Vietnamese descent. He told Do that he was looking to buy 100 kilos of cocaine every month in the U.S., which Dolic's gang would smuggle to Toronto. Dolic called himself "the big wheel" in the illegal drug trade and said he had been doing this for years. He mentioned his involvement in a huge shipment of hash that police had seized in the 1980s and boasted that the members of his gang "do the time" if caught, never ratting on him. He bragged about his "$1.5 million house."

The two dealers agreed to do business. Dolic would send money to Do as a down payment on 30 kilograms of cocaine. (At this time, Dolic usually paid about $12,000 a kilo.) It was agreed that the loads from Do to Dolic would later increase to 100 kilos a month. Dolic gave instructions on how the cocaine was to be put in a spare tire and given to a member of his gang in Buffalo.

Dolic was unaware that Thoi Uc Do had recently been arrested in Houston by the U.S. Drug Enforcement Agency and had become a "cooperating defendant," helping the DEA to arrest other dealers. Do told the DEA that Dolic was trafficking drugs in Houston — in fact, the DEA had recorded the telephone conversation between the two men. Although Dolic worked from Ontario and had never been to Texas, the Houston branch of the DEA had jurisdiction to investigate and charge him, as the illegal transactions were to occur in that state.

On January 12, 2006, in Chicago, a member of Dolic's gang delivered a $177,300 cash down payment to one of Do's associates. And in Buffalo, another Dolic gang member met Do, who gave him a spare tire containing cocaine. As Dolic's minion was leaving, he was arrested and the tire was seized.

Dolic quickly heard about the arrest and seizure — he phoned Do and told him. According to their agreement, the seized cocaine still had to be paid for. In Baltimore, a member of Dolic's gang gave an undercover DEA agent $193,030 — the balance left after the $177,300 down payment — in cash for Do's shipment.

In March 2006, an undercover agent in Houston, posing as a cocaine distributor, contacted Dolic and learned about two men he used for smuggling drugs. Dolic introduced the smugglers to the undercover agent, who gave them 45 kilos of cocaine to smuggle to Dolic. After the meeting, the police arrested the smugglers and seized the cocaine. But before Dolic learned of the latest arrests and seizure, the undercover agent phoned Dolic and said the transfer had been successful. Dolic told the undercover officer to pick up a "paycheck" in Dallas for "300." That day, two members of Dolic's gang gave $295,750 in cash to an undercover agent in Dallas.

On October 26, 2006, a U.S. federal grand jury indicted Drago Dolic — along with 15 others — for "conspiracy to possess with intent to distribute marijuana and conspiracy to launder money." Cocaine charges would be added later.

Dolic was in Mississauga at the time and did not know of the secret indictment, or that the U.S. government was planning to reach over the border to grab him. In December, he married a much younger, beautiful, curvy brunette. He was sober, healthy and rich (both in friendships and in money), and he loved his new family — he had found happiness.

Also indicted were two of Dolic's minions — Serge and Diana Bernier, the retired Quebecois couple who spent their retirement years traveling around with a camper trailer hitched behind their car, funding their lifestyle by smuggling drugs and money for Drago Dolic. Since 2002, the Berniers had been buying multi-kilogram loads of cocaine from different parts of the U.S. and hauling it to Minnesota or New York State, where others in Dolic's gang would take it over the border to Ontario, bound for Toronto.

On Valentine's Day, 2007, two months after Dolic's wedding, he sent the Berniers to Brownsville to buy 14 to 15 kilos of cocaine from another drug dealer who was cooperating with the DEA. The retired couple went into a residential house, where they were videotaped looking at 25 one-kilo bags of cocaine and then cutting open four bags, tasting small amounts. They also each inhaled a bit up their noses. The Berniers told the DEA's cooperating defendant that they would like to look at different cocaine, left the house and returned two hours later to examine another 25 kilos. None of it was of good quality, they apparently decided. They said they did not want to buy anything they had sampled that day, but that they would return the next day to examine some different cocaine.

The Berniers drove their trailer camper to a trailer park in Harlingen, Texas, and as soon as they got out of their car, they were arrested. A search of their trailer turned up $174,000 in cash, and the Berniers admitted the money was for buying cocaine. They told the officers about Dolic and his "Asian connection," which was led by a man nicknamed "Uncle Bob." The U.S. government asked the

Canadian federal government to arrest Drago Dolic and send him to the U.S. for prosecution.

At the time, the newlywed Dolic was busy setting up a massive new grow op near Toronto's Pearson International Airport, a location he chose because, for safety reasons, police helicopters were not allowed to fly near it. On November 16, 2007, 13 months after he was indicted, Dolic was arrested by Canadian police and flown to Houston to face prosecution. At 48 years of age, he was looking at decades in prison.

Two days after Dolic pled not guilty, his second child — another daughter — was born. A couple of years later, hoping for sympathy and leniency, he reversed his plea in a letter to the judge:

> *Dolic — #82508-179*
> *Federal Detention Center*
> *PO Box 526255*
> *Houston, TX*
> *77052-6255*
>
> *YOUR HONOR*
> *Judge Lynn N. Hughes*
>   *Please accept my guilty plea. Today was a very difficult day for me in my life. My wife who I love very much has decided to move on with her life because she sees no future with me. My wife . . . and our two children [the newborn daughter and his wife's daughter from a previous relationship]. . . do love me very much and it must of been very hard for her and our children in the last two years of my lock up. My wife is twenty-nine years old and said twenty years is a life time and made a hard decision to make a new life for her and her children. God knows how much they mean to me and how much I love then, I must accept the out-come because of my actions. It's hard to even comment.*
>   *I have been locked up for two years this July 4th, it's so hard to explain how I feel today because my world really has fallen to*

pieces and if you could just move me through your court system
as soon as you possibly can I could go and serve out this sentence.
I'm sorry for all the trouble and problems I've caused your country,
you sir and my family. I wish many things but I will have to live
through all of this One Day at a time.

 Thank you

 Drago Dolic

In 2009, Dolic stood in court and pled guilty to dealing 80 kilograms of cocaine and laundering $1 million. Awaiting sentencing, he did not change his ways. During phone conversations with members of his gang, Dolic would constantly try to involve them in new drug-trafficking schemes that he thought up behind bars.

Bleich would later say that Dolic was so blatant in talking about drug deals in his phone calls from prison that he would have to hang up — the only way to stop Dolic from saying incriminating things on prison phone lines that were routinely bugged. Despite such communication issues, Dolic and Bleich made an arrangement whereby Bleich bought cannabis from Dolic's supplier in Niagara Falls and sold it to Dolic's clients, acting as Dolic's agent. Bleich also had some buyers of his own — guys he had met while in prison for convictions related to the Barrie grow op. The two men split the profit of all Bleich's cannabis capitalism 50–50 and Bleich gave Dolic's share to one of Dolic's relatives. Bleich delivered $3,000 to $10,000 to Dolic's relative every month, and an additional $500 a month to Dolic himself.

Dolic was also in contact with Glenn Day through mail and email. He asked Day for $250 a month, which Day agreed to send to his imprisoned boss and friend.

Serge and Diana Bernier, who had helped build the case against Drago Dolic in hope of seeing reductions in their own prison sentences for trafficking, also wrote letters to the judge.

Diana Bernier — prisoner #70952-179 — wrote (with spelling and punctuation corrected):

Your Honor

I was born in Gaspé, Quebec, Canada, on Nov. 4, 1944. I lived mostly with my paternal grandparents. My grandfather had cancer of the face after having a mole removed. We had to go to Montreal city, where he was treated at the General Hospital. I had to quit school in the 7th grade, to get work to help my grandmother pay the bills.

I met my husband Serge in July 1962. It was fun dating him. He was a real gentleman. I couldn't speak French and he couldn't speak English. We would take a pen and paper on our dates and write each other. He could read English very well. He learned to speak English a lot faster than I learned French. It was as if we knew each other well from day one.

We got married on Aug 31, 1963. We had 3 children, a boy in 1964, a girl in 1967 and another girl in 1976 . . .

I used to smoke cigarettes when we met. Serge made me see how bad it was for me. I quit after dating him a few days . . .

We have never been people to party. We never in our lives drank anything with alcohol in it. Serge would tell people we were too young. He still says that . . . We don't smoke and we can count on one hand how many times we've been to a bar. We can say the same for our children and their spouses . . .

We have always been spiritual people. We love, believe and respect God, Jesus and the Mother Mary. We try to do what they suggest we do . . .

We worked for the J. D. Irving Company in the forest for many years. We are honest . . . We also bought wood lots and got the wood out.

It is in our character to help people who have fallen on hard times, if we can. However, the things I have seen and have been subjected to in the last 19 months . . . have opened my eyes and shown me a lot of other people's character. We are very trusting people and that has gotten us where we are today . . .

I'm a wife and a mother and a grandmother who is sincerely sorry for my mistakes. The time that I have left with my family is sacred to me and I would not ever put that in jeopardy again.

Thank you for this time to be able to give you an idea of my true nature.

Sincerely,

Diana Bernier

Serge Bernier — prisoner #70951-179 — wrote two letters to the judge (with spelling and punctuation corrected):

Honorable Judge Lynn N. Hughes

We have a close and peaceful family, there was never any fighting amongst us, or with anyone else, not even in the school years. We grew up in a very small town where most people knew each other. With the exception of my brother, Yvon, none of the family even drank alcohol or smoked. I am the youngest of 8 children . . .

The rest of the letter was a list of various family members, describing how and when each had died.

Serge's second letter began:

Honorable Judge Lynn Hughes

Hi, Your Honor, only a few words. This is the first letter I wrote in about 50 years, except to Diana the last 32 months. First, Your Honor, I would like to thank you for making her feel at ease in your court. I know she was a nervous wreck, especially because I was not by her side. She never had these kinds of problems before, not even a ticket. I was also very nervous [and] I had been told not to say a word except guilty . . . Give my thanks to [the prosecutor] for not trying to take our home and to release our airplane. I am sure by now he knows we had no drug money in anything we owned . . .

The money I earned transporting drugs . . . was used to help people — most of them pure strangers. I know it may sound pretty hard to believe, but it is the truth . . . I would also like to give my thanks to all the personnel at the [Federal Detention Centre]. You can't ask for a better group of people . . . all so polite and always helpful. The food is good, always on time and the place is super clean.

. . . Not to take too much of Your Honor's time, I will say, I am very sorry for all this mess. To you and everyone concerned, including the working people that have to pay to keep us in here. I know that money could be spent on much better things . . .

I wish Your Honor and your family a beautiful, harmonious and peaceful life, especially when the time arrives to leave this body for the next one. May the transition be very peaceful.

I wish the same for [the prosecutor] and his family . . .

Like I tell my kids, love is overrated. All I want is harmony and thanks to God, Jesus, Mary, their friends and helpers. We have it even here in prison. And if I may, I would like to say to all of you, don't work too hard, take time to enjoy your family and let them enjoy you too. We will all be gone and there will still be work. Courts, inmates and prisons with all their negativity. Like my mother used to say, "Do the right thing, this little life is very short and sometimes shorter." She died at 89.

Your Honor, in closing, I thank you for your time and patience . . . May God, Jesus, Mary and their friends and helpers bless you all and provide you with their help in times of need. Hopefully, you never do, but rest assured, they are there for the asking. Those words are not meaningless, they are my true wishes.

Yours Truly Always,
Serge Bernier

Diana Bernier — who had been infected with hepatitis B at a Houston jail — and her husband were each sentenced to time served, fined $100 and set free.

. . . .

In 1985, U.S. president Ronald Reagan — whose wife, Nancy Reagan, popularized the "Just Say No" anti-drug mantra — had appointed Texas-born Lynn Hughes to the U.S. District Court. According to CNN, Hughes was a "tough but fair" judge, with some controversy over his links to the oil industry.

On the afternoon of January 4, 2010, Judge Hughes said, "Mr. Dolic, is there anything you would like to tell me, please, sir, before I sentence you?"

"Yes, Your Honour," Dolic said. "I have been here for quite a few years. I wrote you a letter because I just wanted to move on with my life and, you know, try to deal with the issue on hand. It was a difficult day to write the letter. I really wanted to say thank you for accepting my letter and getting me in front of you. I remember writing the letter on the third and you received it on the sixth and on the 13th of July, I was here in front of you. It was like magical all of a sudden because, for years, it just seemed like nobody had heard me. I just wanted to get in here and get this part of my life over with. And I appreciate the fact that you got me here promptly and we get to deal with the issue on hand.

"Mr. Nugent [a defense lawyer] mentioned my family. He mentioned my father passing away. That was May of '08. At least I talked to him. That was a good thing.

"My father and I were very close . . . we did get into some arguments when I was in my 20s and 30s. I made my amends and made my peace with my father and we became best of friends and I wish I was there, being the oldest son, to bury him. My actions brought me to a different place in my life. Talking to him on the phone the night before he passed away, I said to him, 'I'm glad we said our sorries a long time ago to each other.' He said, 'Yeah.' I said, 'We had a pretty good time of it.' He said, 'We got through that.' And the next day he passed away.

"That whole time, I just kept wanting to come to court and just plead guilty, get out of here, point blank, that's the way it is.

"And when I wrote that letter, my wife and I, you know, we were going through some rough times. She loves me and I love her and I love the two children. I love them with all of my heart.

"We got married four years ago, December 17, and it was a very happy day in my life and it was nice to have a child with her. Our oldest one . . . I got to spend a lot of time with her. I have a daughter 16 years old and I never got to spend a lot of time, other than weekends, with her. And finally, you know, I have a wife and a child and we have a home. It was nice to spend time every day with the little girl. I'm getting up in age. It was nice to have some responsibility at home. We had another child . . . I came to prison July 4 of 2007 and my daughter was born November 23. It was also a very happy day. I just didn't like where I was, but it was a very happy day.

"I . . . really don't know how to say sorry to my wife. I don't know where to begin. My wife is here today. If you don't mind, I would like to say sorry to my wife, if you don't mind me turning around and just telling her for one minute."

"That is who you ought to say sorry to," the judge said.

Dolic turned toward his wife in the Texas courtroom. "I hurt you in so many ways, and the children," he said. "I want to say I'm truly sorry. I love you and I don't want my life here. I'm really sorry." Weeping, Dolic faced the judge again. "Your Honor, I apologize. I'm not usually a train wreck, but today —"

Judge: "As you have known for two and a half years, you are in deep trouble."

Dolic: "I didn't think I was going to fall apart, Your Honor. Not today. I thought after being here so long, being locked up, you start to question yourself, you think you are getting colder and that, you know, you will be able to face the judge and whatever happens, no tears, you walk in there, walk out, it will be fine. When I came into the courtroom and I seen my wife today, which I hardly ever see, I was falling apart. And I apologize for falling apart. I'm trying."

Judge: "That's all right. Mr. Dolic, people like her are the reason why you don't do what you did."

Dolic: "I understand that."

Judge: "You are missing a lot. That's the nature of losing your freedom . . . It's sad. It's a loss to you. It's a loss to your daughters, to your wife, to your friends, family. It's a loss to your neighbours who can use a hardworking, thrifty, bill-paying, responsible person, instead of huge amounts of costs by your government and ours, lawyers all over the place, all so a bunch of nuts in Toronto could have a little cocaine and destroy their lives. And, conversely, people in Houston smoke cheaper dope, not a very useful enterprise to risk your life and your freedom. The problem is that you were better at it than most, apparently, because you recruited a bunch of capable couriers . . . You are the one who had the contacts, gave instructions, recruited, paid. And you're a leader . . . You don't want your little girl choosing dope, do you?"

Dolic: "No, sir."

Judge: "You don't want people using dope to be around her, but all of those drugs went to somebody's children. Everybody is somebody's child, but not only that, people who were around children, driving, at least on this end of the transaction, possessing guns nine out of ten times. The other harm you did was to a bunch of people who without your inducements were not likely to have become a serious criminal. You are responsible for the harm you've done to them and their loved ones. Yes, they were grown-ups. Yes, they chose to do it. Yes, they did it intentionally . . . I'm not excusing their conduct. But without a leader, none of these people would have been involved in this case at the level they were involved. Any one of them could walk out on the street outside the courthouse and deal in consumer quantities of drugs. It's a lot harder to arbitrage cocaine and marijuana and shift the money back and forth. Mr. Dolic, I sentence you to 324 months [27 years]."

Hughes also ordered all of Dolic's property in Canada to be forfeited.

At the end of the hearing, Dolic's defense lawyer said, "Judge — I know I am probably overstepping — but Mrs. Dolic came in last night. She arrived around midnight. Today is a visitation day at the

Federal Detention Center. They are going to miss that today. I know that the marshals aren't able to have her visit upstairs. If the court would allow him to visit with his wife for five minutes today at the end of your hearings. If that is possible, I ask the court to do that just so that she has a chance to visit with him."

"I inquired into that and I am sorry," the judge replied. "Mr. Dolic, I want people to love you. I want your children to build a relationship, however strained it is going to be. But we have our security problems. Today is a bad day because a [court security officer] in Las Vegas was shot and killed by somebody at the screening station, so we are not doing things we might do on a slow day . . . Oh, and there's anthrax in two courthouses in Alabama. Other than that, I would agree to your request. Ma'am, I'm sorry. It is just not possible under the circumstances."

Dolic was led from the courtroom. He went to a nine-month-old medium-security prison in forest surroundings in Pollock, Louisiana, where he was the only Canadian. He was able to continue with his Alcoholics Anonymous program there. Dolic communicated with Glenn Day, thanking Day for sending money and discussing Dolic's hopes to be transferred to a prison in Pennsylvania, a 90-minute drive south of Buffalo — a much easier visit for his family.

Although Dolic could not access the internet in prison, his family helped him set up a Facebook account, and posted his contact information. In the "About Drago" section, someone posted for him:

to send mail:
[address]

to send money:
WESTERN UNION (quick transactions)
[wiring instructions]

Money orders by mail are the best. Mail to:
FEDERAL BUREAU OF PRISONS

DRAGO DOLIC #82508-179
[address]

I'm looking for my daughter, Katherine . . . Last seen my daughter when she was 3 and a half, in the city of Elliot Lake, Ontario. She is 21 now, born April 19, 1989. Please write to me if you find this. Love you and miss you. Love your Dad, Dan Dolic.

A later post on Dolic's Facebook page read:

Please write to me, I will update any address changes here. If you would like to contribute any financial support that would be greatly appreciated. This will go to email, phone and some food and jean supply. Hope to return to Canada to be with my family and friends in the future. Love always, Dan XOXO

Eventually, Day's application to visit Dolic was approved. Dolic emailed the news to Day, providing a visitation schedule, a description of several hotels near the prison and a list of things to do in the nearby town.

Dolic would not have been so enthusiastic if he had known that Glenn Day — just like Thoi Uc Do — had agreed to work for the police.

Briefing

Cannabis can be grown either indoors (in a grow op) or outdoors (on a farm).

Dolic, Bleich and the rest of the gang were experienced with both methods.

Outdoor gardeners plant seeds or babies in somebody else's field of corn or a dry area in a swamp or deep in a trackless forest.

Outdoor gardening is cheaper and often presents less risk of arrest.

But outdoor gardening has several disadvantages: reduced control over the environment, visibility to aircraft, the need to travel to out-of-the-way areas — and, most stressful of all, theft.

Some of the theft is by nibbling mammals: deer, rabbits, mice, raccoons, squirrels, etc.

Some is by swarming bugs: leafhoppers, treehoppers, cucumber beetles, thrips, flea beetles, caterpillars, snails, slugs, mites, aphids, etc.

Some is by people.

Cannabis thieves locate outdoor crops through espionage (picking up gossip and getting people to talk too much), through airplane reconnaissance, through searching likely areas on foot or through dumb luck, while out hunting or hiking.

Having located somebody else's outdoor garden, a cannabis thief estimates the date when the crop should be ready for harvest. Shortly before that date, the thief returns — possibly armed, in case the owners of the crop happen to show up. Some cannabis thieves carry machetes, both for self-protection and for cutting down their heist. They also have to watch out for booby traps, which can take many forms: IEDs, guns set up to fire when a wire is touched or a laser beam broken, holes in the ground filled with spikes, triple-pronged fish hooks hanging on lines at eye level, falling logs or boulders, leg-chomping steel jaws, chemical sprays, etc. Some use vicious guard dogs. And some outdoor growers choose locations infested with mosquitoes, wasps, skunks or poison ivy.

Despite the risks, stealing cannabis is very popular in North America.

Slaves of Ontario

"Don't you guys know that I spent $4,000 to get you?"
— Bob DeRosa

Manila, the Philippines, 2006.

Edwin Canilang, a skilled welder, noticed an advertisement for work in Canada, building ocean-going icebreakers. The pay was $23 an hour, plus food, lodging and overtime. Canilang was interested. He contacted a local recruiting company to apply for one of the positions. After undergoing medical tests, upgrading their technical skills and taking English lessons, all at their own expense, Canilang and 10 other Filipino men were offered positions as temporary foreign workers in Canada — for a fee of $12,500 paid to the recruiting company, supposedly to cover work permits and airfare. Some of the newly hired men borrowed money at high interest rates or sold all their belongings to meet the payment.

All of them now deeply in debt, they quit their jobs at home and said goodbye to their friends and families. For Canilang, leaving his family behind was especially difficult — his wife was pregnant with their third child.

On June 29, 2007, eight of the Filipino men flew into Toronto's Pearson International Airport. Expecting a representative from the shipbuilding company, they were instead met at the airport by Sharon Baal,★ an employee of the Manila-based recruiting company. Baal — of Filipino descent, a citizen of Taiwan, currently in Canada on a visitor's visa — crammed the eight men into two taxis and took them to a house near Scarborough's Pacific Mall. A few days later, three more Filipino workers arrived at the house.

Baal told the 11 men that they would live in two rooms in the basement. There were no telephones in the house. She took away their work permits and passports, and told them they were not allowed to contact their relatives back in the Philippines.

Canilang later recalled, "We slept four people to a bed. It was awful."

After a week, Baal told the men that the work on the icebreakers was no longer available. They would have to relocate and work for a different company. Baal and an associate (who falsely claimed to be a lawyer) drove the 11 Filipinos north for two hours to Elmvale, a small town near Wasaga Beach.

On a country road just outside of Elmvale, Baal stopped at an abandoned green and white farmhouse. Getting out of the vehicle, Canilang and the others were introduced by Baal to Bob DeRosa, who said, "This is your new home, boys."

Baal and the fake lawyer left, and DeRosa showed the men their rundown, dirty new home. They were to sleep on mattresses with soiled sheets. The fridge was empty. The towels in the bathroom were filthy. The whole place was filthy. The central Ontario location was isolated and, to Filipino eyes, alien.

One of the workers later said, "Outside, the grass was five feet tall. Inside, there was mud on the floor everywhere. We had to spend a week cleaning it up."

Telling the Filipinos they would be paid later, DeRosa assigned them work at various places around central and southern Ontario. Some of their work took place at DeRosa's farmhouse, where the trained welders and plumbers were ordered to dig ditches or pick up garbage. One of the workplaces was Aurora Beverage, the water-bottling company owned by Vincent DeRosa that rented space at the Molson property in Barrie.

The men started at 5:15 a.m. and worked very long days. At least one worker, Narciso Nicdao, was forced to work a 24-hour shift at Aurora Beverage, cleaning out a "beer cage." Another, Ronald Galang, had to work 17 days in a row without a day off, dividing his time between Aurora Beverage and a factory in Orillia. Two men were assigned work at a DeRosa-linked brewery in southern Ontario, close to the border with New York State. None of the work involved plumbing or welding, their skills. Much of it was menial.

Bob DeRosa would sometimes bring food to the men at the Elmvale farmhouse: once he delivered pasta and tomatoes, another time buffalo meat. During their infrequent free time, the men watched TV on an old black-and-white set with a rabbit-ear antenna. They built a pool table from pieces of scrap wood and fixed the tires on some kids' bikes they found in a shed, riding them on a dirt road near the farmhouse.

Two weeks after arriving in Canada, the unhappy group of foreign men crossed the road and approached a neighbouring farmhouse. They spoke with the neighbour — George Cabral, a Barrie police sergeant — who later said, "They were strangers in this country, isolated, without a phone." The kindhearted Cabral drove two of the men into Elmvale, where he bought them a meal and gave them money for phone cards.

In early August, 2007, after six weeks in Canada, Edwin Canilang was in the back of a van with four other Filipino men at 5:30 a.m., heading toward Aurora Beverages in Barrie. Canilang and some of the others were to spend another day cleaning up there.

Canilang missed his family and hated his new life in Canada. Back in San Carlos, north of Manila, Canilang's wife had just given birth to their third child.

As the van jolted down a bumpy dirt road, Canilang leaned forward and asked Bob DeRosa when they would get their first paycheck.

"Don't you guys know that I spent $4,000 to get you?" Bob DeRosa replied.

It was then that Canilang realized they had been bought and sold. They were slaves.

DeRosa never paid them the money he had promised. He often threatened to have them deported. Sometimes, when they complained, he would give them small amounts of cash. For six weeks of hard, exhausting, dirty labor, none of the men were paid more than $900, and one received only $200.

The owner of the Orillia factory — which was not connected to the DeRosa family — would later say he had paid Bob DeRosa for the services of the two men DeRosa had subcontracted to him: "All I know is that I paid off all my bills. If they didn't get paid, I guess they have to go after Bob."

In late August, Filipino welder Eric Martinez had had enough. He found a way to phone the Filipino consulate and told them how he and the others were being exploited. Soon after that conversation, Martinez escaped from a work site near Hamilton. He eventually met a Canadian of Filipino descent, who took pity on Martinez and gave him a ride to Charlottetown, Prince Edward Island, in the Canadian Maritimes. Martinez lost contact with the Filipino consulate but a few days after his escape, by coincidence, most of the members of that consulate travelled to the East Coast and held a public meeting in Charlottetown. Martinez attended the meeting and, hearing a consular officer talk about exploited Filipino workers, Martinez put up his hand and said he had suffered such treatment himself back in Hamilton and that there were other workers still trapped in Elmvale. The Filipino diplomats took Martinez back to Toronto.

On Monday, August 21, 2007, without calling the police first, the staff of the consulate tried to locate the Elmvale farmhouse. Martinez told them it was on Floss Road, but there were many Floss Roads in the Wasaga Beach/Barrie area. The staff drove Martinez around in a van for much of the day, searching for the right location. For a while, their vehicle was followed by another van. (It is still a mystery who was driving the second van.) They finally found the farmhouse when Martinez recognized the clothes hanging on an outdoor clothesline.

When night fell, Martinez and the Filipino consular staff approached the farmhouse and met with the remaining Filipino workers there. A consular officer asked if they wanted to leave, and they said they wanted to stay a bit longer so they could get the pay they'd been promised for all their hard, menial labor. The consular staff agreed to come back for them three days later, on Thursday.

On Wednesday, the Filipino workers told Bob DeRosa they refused to work for him anymore, and DeRosa flew into a rage. "I am warning you for the last time!" he shouted at them. When his human property continued to defy him, DeRosa said he was going to sign a deportation order and stormed off the property.

Immediately afterwards, staff from the Filipino consulate received a phone call from the Elmvale workers, who described what had just happened. Two hours after Bob DeRosa's furious exit, consular staff showed up en masse at the Elmvale farmhouse, emancipating the slaves. Reunited with Martinez, the group was nicknamed by the media "the Elmvale 11."

Dale Brazao of the *Toronto Star* tried repeatedly to secure an interview with Bob DeRosa; finally, DeRosa sent the reporter an email: *"No comment. Please stop calling."*

Sharon Baal, of the Filipino recruiting company, also refused to comment.

A memo from a Filipino employment recruiter suggested that the fake lawyer who had helped deliver the 11 workers to Elmvale had been paid "one thousand per head" for signing up workers in Manila and was to receive another $1,000 for each worker who arrived in Canada. The fake lawyer denied receiving any such payments. He told Brazao he had arranged jobs for the Elmvale 11 "from the goodness of my heart. Bob DeRosa asked me if I know any workers. I know this one girl [Baal] had some workers. So I put them together, that's all."

Brazao's article in the *Star* quoted Edwin Canilang saying, "We didn't believe such scum existed here. Canada has such a great reputation worldwide." But Canilang still hoped that DeRosa would pay the rest of the promised money, adding, "Even slaves have some rights!"

A week after losing his Filipino slaves, Bob DeRosa applied to the federal government for work permits to import 191 more temporary foreign workers to Canada, supposedly for a big construction project. The foreign workers, he wrote, would be paid $18 to $28 an hour, plus full benefits.

The government said no.

Members of the Elmvale 11 moved to Saskatchewan, Alberta and British Columbia and got much better jobs.

No criminal charges were laid.

After the *Star* article appeared, the DeRosa brothers had a big argument. Vincent was upset about the slavery scandal and how the article incorrectly described Bob as a co-owner of the Molson plant. He later called the article "the last straw."

Vincent stopped supporting Bob financially and cut off almost all contact with his older brother; they would see each other only at family functions.

Briefing

Two perspectives on police informants (also known as "snitches," "finks" and "rats").

1) Canadian Case Law

To form the grounds of arrest warrant or search warrant, information from an informant must be carefully considered based on: 1. the degree of detail provided; 2. the informant's source of information; 3. the informant's past reliability. — *R. v. Warford* (2001), 161 CCC 309

Detail. A high level of detail indicates that the tip "is based on more than mere rumour or gossip." Details should include the length of discussions with the informant, the amount of information presented about the accused and whether the information includes the location of an alleged criminal offence and the kind and amount of drugs alleged to be involved. It is not sufficient to rely on conclusory statements without any information on the "source or means of knowledge and whether there are any indicia of his or her reliability, such as the supplying of reliable information in the past or confirmation of part of his or her story by police surveillance." — *R. v. Greffe* (1990), 1 SCR 755

Source. Hearsay from an informant can be sufficient grounds for arrest or search. — *R. v. Garofoly* (1990), SCJ No. 115

Reliability. Factors to consider when determining an informant's reliability: how long he or she has been known by police; how frequently he or she has been in contact with the police; the number of times that he or she has been paid; the number of valid search warrants that have been based on his or her information; the amount of drugs or money or weapons seized based on his or her information; the number of convictions based on his or her information; the amount of false information provided by the informant; the number of charges laid on the basis of the informant's information that failed to lead to convictions; whether the informant is facing criminal charges when he or she provides the information; whether the informant has a criminal record, particularly for offences of dishonesty (e.g., fraud, obstruction of justice, perjury). — *R. v. Garofoly* (1990), SCJ No. 115

. . . .

2) The New Testament, Matthew 26:14 - 27:5

Then one of the Twelve — the one called Judas Iscariot — went to the chief priests and asked, "What are you willing to give me if I deliver him over to you?" So they counted out for him thirty pieces of silver. From then on Judas watched for an opportunity to hand him over . . .

Now the betrayer had arranged a signal with them: "The one I kiss is the man; arrest him." Going at once to Jesus, Judas said, "Greetings, Rabbi!" and kissed him.

Jesus replied, "Do what you came for, friend."

Then the men stepped forward, seized Jesus and arrested him . . .

When Judas, who had betrayed him, saw that Jesus was condemned, he was seized with remorse and returned the thirty pieces of silver to the chief priests and the elders. "I have sinned," he said, "for I have betrayed innocent blood."

"What is that to us?" they replied. "That's your responsibility."

So Judas threw the money into the temple and left.

Masks and Mirrors

"I did not once sell anybody down the drain."
— Fercan maintenance man Larry McGee

In the summer of 2009, Glenn Day was arrested.

In exchange for the police dropping charges — and for a sum of money — Day agreed to become an informant. An OPP detective sergeant handed Day a "Service Provider Agreement" for an investigation that had been randomly named "Project Birmingham," whose goal was to arrest the masterminds behind the big Barrie grow op. The officer explained the document to Day, who reviewed it. The deal promised him $2,000 a week for at least 16 months, plus expenses, plus generous bonuses if certain results occurred. It also gave him immunity from prosecution — as long as he always told the truth.

Day signed, and would eventually be paid hundreds of thousands of dollars, courtesy of the taxpayers of Ontario, as the centerpiece of Project Birmingham.

A few days later, the on-the-record questioning began. The police officer showed Day a photograph of a man. Day identified him as Drago Dolic and said his nickname was "The Head." Dolic, he said, was in charge of the grow ops at Molson, Oro and Ssonix and was the head of the gang — he did not think there were any moneymen or bosses above Dolic.

He also identified as masterminds Jeff "The Frenchman" DaSilva, Robert "Long-Legs" Bleich, Fred "Goggles" Freeman, Bob "The Deaf Guy" DeRosa and Denis "No Known Nickname" Hould. Day told the police in detail about illegal activities these men and others had been involved in, as well as gossip that Day had heard at meetings at the massage parlour and pricey restaurants.

Day told the OPP about a recent meeting he had with Freeman, who'd wanted to sell some cannabis to Day. He had given Day a sample, saying it was one of the same strains that had been grown at the Barrie grow op. Day had asked Freeman about Jeff DaSilva, the grow-op electrician from Montreal. They also talked about how DaSilva's two sons were both very talented competitive motocross riders. Freeman told Day that Bleich — the only grow-op manager to go to prison over Molson — was in contact with DaSilva and would have his phone number, and that Bleich now lived in Wasaga Beach, running two legitimate businesses, a company called All of the Above that did landscaping, construction and tree-cutting, and another, California Shutters, that sold venetian blinds.

The OPP wanted Day to contact Dolic's sister, Davorka "Dove" Pelikan. Day did not have her phone number, but managed to track her down and contact her. Following his handlers' script, he asked Pelikan if she would be interested in doing some trimming. Pelikan eagerly said yes and told Day how much product she could handle. In a subsequent conversation, she said she could not do any work involving travel to the U.S., as her brother had not yet been sentenced and the U.S. authorities might arrest her as a way of putting pressure on him to become an informant.

Acting again on the instructions of the OPP — as would always be the case from then on — Day contacted Bleich and agreed to meet him at a residential construction site in the Toronto area. Day would be wearing a hidden tape recorder. Before this spying mission, his police handler asked him the usual series of questions, including, "Do you have any safety concerns dealing with the identified targets today?" Day said, as he always did, "No."

On July 13, 2009, Bleich parked his gray, four-door Toyota pickup at a construction site in the Greater Toronto Area and the two men talked. Their conversation ranged from legitimate construction business to illegal drug deals. Bleich told Day that Freeman had a contact in the Niagara Falls area — an Italian guy, Bleich said, who owned the Molson building in Barrie.

Based on information Day extracted for the OPP, Judge McCready of the Ontario Court of Justice issued a wiretap order for Freeman, DaSilva, Pelikan, Hould, Bleich, Dolic and a few others. From this time on, much of their phone, email and text communications could be intercepted.

On August 25, Glenn Day and Constable Terry Richardson, who was posing as an underworld figure, picked up Pelikan in a silver Cadillac at her home in Mississauga, near Square One Mall. They drove east to the Fox and Fiddle restaurant in Toronto, where they sat on the patio, enjoying the warm August weather. Pelikan, the only one of the trio not wearing a hidden tape recorder, spoke of working at Molson for two years. She said she could recruit a team of trimmers, including a "girlfriend" who had also worked at Molson and Oro, as well as that person's mother and one of Pelikan's relatives.

She said that she missed the excitement of trimming and that the money had paid for one of her children to go to university, which had cost $25,000 plus room and board. She also mentioned that she still had some cannabis resin (from scissors and fingers) from Molson at home — some of it "in balls," some "loose" — and that it was still good. She joked that she should have brought some of the resin to share with Day and Richardson. She agreed to get get all of her trimming supplies ready and asked when she could start.

They drove her back home in the silver Cadillac, with plans to go into business together.

Next up, Day phoned Denis Hould, the Molson manager who — warned by Michael DiCicco — had managed to get his crew of six men out of the Molson building before the raid. Hould, an ex-miner from Sudbury with a criminal record for drug trafficking, told Day, "I know my stuff . . . 10 years under my hat. I know all the ins and outs."

Day arranged for Hould to meet with Day's "associate" — an undercover police officer — regarding a big drug purchase.

The following day, Day went to Fred Freeman's house. They discussed Dolic, who had pled guilty and was awaiting sentencing. They talked about how Dolic's father had died while Dolic was in custody, and about Dolic's wife. Freeman told Day of a mutual associate whose grow op had been raided by police and who had "got caught with 40 lights or something," while another man involved in this grow op, a relative of Dolic's, had been arrested by police while he was running down the street, clutching garbage bags filled with cannabis.

At the end of his meeting with Freeman, Day asked if Freeman "had any weed."

"No, not yet, still not ready," Freeman said. He would call Day when he had the cannabis.

. . . .

A few days later, Day met with Denis Hould at a restaurant. Hould told a few stories about working at Molson and other grow ops. Detective Constable Mark Sanders, posing as an underworld figure linked to Day, arrived at the restaurant and was introduced to Hould. Soon, Hould was bragging about how he had driven the minivan full of growers out of the Molson plant and was followed by police to a Tim Hortons, and how when he drove away south along Highway 400 the police were no longer behind him. He told another story about how he had more recently tried to bring 150 pounds of cannabis from Vancouver to Ontario, but he had been arrested and the product had been seized.

Day said he and Sanders were going to build a new grow op, hopefully with the help of DaSilva and his crew of Quebecois tradesmen. They asked Hould to be the main guy on-site, and Hould agreed. He estimated that he would be able to produce 2.2 pounds of cannabis per candle, and, to do it right, he would need a baby room, three to four grow rooms and a drying room. He asked where the other workers were coming from.

Sanders said Pelikan would be doing the trimming, and then the two men talked about different strains and how to stagger grow schedules for a consistent yield. Hould said that he was just spending quality time with his two daughters these days and that he was the right man for the job. He even had grow-op supplies.

Hould would later tell Day that his last payday from the Barrie grow op had netted him $75,000. Of that, $48,000 had gone toward buying his house in Elliot Lake. He was grateful for both the money and the opportunity to learn from Bleich and other talented growers.

Asked by the undercover officer about his work running the Barrie Good Fish grow area, Hould said, "I was pretty good at drying them . . . [I had] 600 fucking lights and I had these little cocksuckers working for me. I worked hard there, man . . . We were making good money. It's too bad it didn't last another three years. Fuck, we were doing good. I was doing good. I was putting all my fucking money into the fucking bank, plus my crop. I had 40 pounds [per personal harvest] . . . paying for my gas, my cigarettes, my fucking room down there . . . everything else was going in the fucking bank."

He estimated he had made about $400,000 over two years as the Barrie Good Fish grow-op manager.

The following Tuesday, Constable Sanders phoned Pelikan and said he had some work for her on Thursday. Constable Richardson dropped by Pelikan's Mississauga house two days later and gave her a package, supposedly containing drugs. Her job was to transport the package. They drove to the train station, with Pelikan talking about a medical problem with her knee caused by a car accident. She also talked about her family, traffic congestion, travel, vacations and having to move her trailer out of the trailer park in Wasaga Beach because the site was closing down.

Pelikan took the package on a train to downtown Toronto, where she went to a restaurant and met two undercover police officers — Sanders and John Scott Hogarth — who took the package. Their conversation was wide-ranging. Pelikan told them as well about her bad knee. One of the men suggested renting the Molson plant for another grow op and they all laughed. Pelikan described how she had seen the Barrie raid on the TV news and how "the cops were dumfounded." She talked about special scissors for trimming that had cost her $62. After a discussion about air fresheners in the trimming place and how important it was to hire the right people, Sanders paid Pelikan for smuggling the package from one police officer to another. He also gave her cab fare home.

A week later, at 4:30 p.m., Pelikan met Constable Sanders in Mississauga, at the Tim Hortons at the corner of Dundas Street and Confederation Parkway. They got coffees and sat in Sanders' car. Pelikan said she had three trimmers ready: her "girlfriend," that person's husband and Pelikan's relative, whom she would train. They were all available to do trimming that weekend. Pelikan agreed they would be paid $150 per pound, and Sanders said he wanted all the resin from the scissors and the trimmers' fingertips.

At one point in the conversation, Pelikan asked the undercover officer if he could get her some Percocet pills. He said no.

The trimmers met on September 19 at Glenn Day's place of business for his corporation, a small warehouse in a strip mall in Newmarket. Pelikan had brought her relative and a guy named Allan. They went inside and met with Day and three undercover officers: Richardson, Kaury Jones and Robert Henderson. Day recognized Allan — the two had once worked together for a single day as trimmers at a grow op. Allan told Day he had been too drunk to work that day and had to take a taxi back home to St. Catharines, costing him $300.

The trimmers trimmed and the undercover officers encouraged everybody to talk about the drug business until past 10:30 that night;

it was all caught on videotape. Pelikan complained that she had not done any trimming since Molson and had only had one "shit" job since then.

While scissoring flowers, Pelikan told an undercover officer that her brother was going to plead guilty to his U.S. charges. She said he'd been "ratted out" by a 65-year-old couple — Serge and Diana Bernier — and that Dolic would not rat anybody out. She mentioned that the U.S. authorities hadn't allowed Dolic to come back to Canada for their father's funeral.

The next day, more videotaped trimming took place at Day's place of business. Pelikan mentioned that a member of her family was an electrician and could be trusted for grow-op work. At the end of the day, she gave Henderson a piece of paper with her trimming calculations on it. He handed over $600 in partial payment. Later, Pelikan got $1,200 more from an undercover officer in an undercover police car in the parking lot of Toronto's Yorkdale Mall.

. . . .

Fall 2009.

Robert Bleich — living near Wasaga Beach and still on parole for the Barrie grow-op crimes — had just harvested an outdoor crop. He had started growing again in 2006, as soon as he had been released from the halfway house in Hamilton. For a legitimate source of income, he'd gone back to tree removal and landscape work, sometimes for his own customers, sometimes helping out his uncle. It was dangerous work — there were risks of falling from a height, getting cut by a tool or having a tree or a big branch fall down on him.

Bleich did some occasional tree removal work as a subcontractor for Glenn Day. Their paths also happened to cross when they were both working at the house of Pierre Homard, the man they'd built a grow op for in Kawartha Lakes. (Tipped off by Glenn Day, OPP officers would later arrest Homard for several cannabis related offences, but he would be acquitted of all charges.)

"Glenn Day was trying to pull me [into the police investigation] with offers of work and getting me to talk when he was wired," Bleich later recalled. "One day at a site, he asked for some weed. He said he knew someone in construction who might want 10 pounds . . . Everyone in construction smokes . . . [The construction industry] is a good way to wash money."

Bleich told Day on the phone that he had 30 pounds of cannabis for sale at $1,700 a pound. (It was outdoor cannabis, less valuable than indoor; Bleich had bought it for about $1,300 a pound.) They arranged to meet at a Tim Hortons in Wasaga Beach, but when Day arrived, Bleich told him he had already sold the last of the crop.

What about getting product from "The Frenchman"? asked Day.

Bleich said DaSilva was still in the forests and swamps of Quebec, harvesting his outdoor crops, and would not be reachable until after the upcoming long weekend. At that time, Bleich predicted, DaSilva would have stuff to sell.

. . . .

In October 2009, Hould and Day met in Newmarket and then drove around the province, looking at five supposed potential grow-op locations — the addresses had been supplied to Day by the OPP. Afterwards, Hould suggested they drive north to the old Molson plant in Barrie and talk with Bob DeRosa.

When they got there, they parked by some of the stainless-steel brewing tanks that had been dragged out of the half-demolished building. Hould talked about growing cannabis inside those tanks, with 20 candles each and air ducts and an air conditioner inside. As Hould talked about the old grow op, the tape recorder under Day's clothes listened.

Fercan maintenance man Larry McGee showed up after his lunch in an older-model Jeep driven by a woman. He joined Hould and Day and the three men started telling grow-op stories. McGee said the cops had been after him for a whole year after the raid, calling him in six times to be questioned, but he never was charged. He said he was glad he had always worn gloves around the grow ops, so as to not leave behind fingerprints.

Sounding defensive, he declared, "I did not once sell anybody down the drain." He claimed that Vincent DeRosa had "turned his lawyers on right away" and that the police had not been able to talk with him.

McGee said he would work at the Molson site until he was no longer needed there, then he had a job lined up at a boiler company.

Day asked about Bob DeRosa. McGee said that Bob was "out doing his own thing now" and no longer involved with any of his younger brother's real estate holdings. The brothers, he explained, had argued about the way Bob did business, with Vincent accusing his older brother of ripping people off. McGee said Vincent had kicked Bob off the Molson property and had lowered his weekly allowance from $4,000 to $1,000.

McGee also mentioned that Vincent DeRosa owned another $12 million industrial building in the Barrie area, just down Highway 400 from the Molson property: the Bemis factory, which had previously manufactured toilet seats. He said the RCMP had sent an email to Fercan, asking to rent the old Bemis building for three weeks during the 2010 G8 summit, for security and storage. (This arrangement did take place, with Vincent DeRosa's corporation as a landlord to the Harper Conservative government.)

Finally, Day and Hould invited McGee to join them in building and running a new grow op. McGee was enthusiastic, saying he could do all the construction work and electrical wiring.

A few days later, Day got a phone call from Bleich, who said he was in St. Catharines and had "10 hours of work" for Day, which was code for "10 pounds of cannabis." Bleich said he was "bottling wine" and that the address of the bottling place was "1650 Eglinton" — code for "the price is $1,650 a pound."

They agreed to meet at 6:30 p.m. at the Husky Truck Stop halfway between Newmarket and Barrie. Day got to the gas station restaurant first and sat down.

When Bleich arrived at the Husky lot, police surveillance watched him take a large cardboard box from a larger locked box in the back of his gray Toyota Tundra pickup. He walked to Day's car, opened the trunk, put the box in and closed the trunk. Bleich then walked to the restaurant and joined Day inside, saying he had 10 pounds and would sell Day 8 pounds and keep two for himself to show people. Bleich asked Day where the money was. Day said it was in his pocket.

Conversation moved on, and Bleich said he was still working with Dolic and that Dolic had recently lost his phone and email use for a time, because he had allowed another inmate to use his phone privileges, which was against the lockup rules.

Bleich said his supplier was from around Niagara Falls and could supply Day with 10 pounds a week until Christmas. He suggested that Day sell the cannabis for $1,800 a pound, to make maximum profits. Bleich said his parole was almost expired and then he would have more flexibility.

After the two men had talked, they left the Husky restaurant and went to Day's car. They drove to a different part of the large parking lot, where Day handed Bleich a paper bag containing $13,200. He asked if Bleich wanted to count it, and Bleich said that he trusted him. He told Day not to be nervous and to make sure he drove the speed limit on his way home, to avoid being pulled over by police.

Day then drove his car to Bleich's Tundra, where Bleich got in and pulled out of the lot.

Police came out of hiding, opened the trunk of Day's car and found what Bleich had left inside: a large cardboard box, printed with the word *Kenmore* and shut with strips of blue tape. Inside the box were eight one-pound shrink-wrapped bags of green cannabis flowers. There were no fingerprints on the Kenmore box or any of the bags. The evidence was videotaped, labeled and sent to storage, until it would be needed in court.

Bleich sold similar amounts to Day on several other occasions. Sometimes they'd meet in the morning and have a breakfast of bacon and eggs first. Day would have coffee too; Bleich never touched coffee.

· · · · · · ·

Three other significant things happened around this time: 1) Day started sending locked-up Dolic $250 a month; 2) Dolic sent Day a form to request an in-person prison visit; and 3) at Halloween, Pelikan suffered her first stroke.

· · · · · · ·

Robert Bleich phoned Glenn Day early in the morning of October 10, 2009, saying in code that 20 pounds of cannabis were available. At one point during the conversation, Day used the word "marijuana" instead of a code word or euphemism, and Bleich quickly corrected him. They made arrangements to meet later at The Keg in Barrie.

Bleich then drove his Tundra to the Walmart in a plaza on Brock Road in Pickering, where he met Yvan Guindon of Montreal, who drove a blue Chevrolet Silverado pickup. Guindon, 54, was five-seven, 185 pounds, with short dark hair. He enjoyed recreational hunting and spoke little English. He was Jeff DaSilva's "runner" — couriering drugs and money for DaSilva and taking on the risk of arrest.

In a brief, near-wordless encounter, Bleich got some cannabis from Guindon and left. He then drove to Wasaga Beach, where he stopped at the home of the recently widowed mother of Dolic and Pelikan and did some work on her trees.

Later, Bleich drove to a car pool parking lot in Barrie, where he met Day. They both got into Day's car and drove south to The Keg on Yonge Street in Newmarket. Constable Mark Sanders was inside the steakhouse. Bleich would later describe Sanders: "tall, bald, skinny, white, in his 40s, wearing a leather coat, cowboy boots, jeans."

All of the men ordered steak for dinner. Bleich — under the impression that Sanders was an underworld figure who employed Day — asked Sanders about the eight pounds of cannabis from the deal at the Husky parking lot. Sanders talked to Bleich about wanting to buy 25 pounds of cannabis; Bleich said he had 22 or 23 pounds, at $1,500 a pound, and would try to find another two pounds for Sanders' order. He explained that he resupplied every two weeks and had four regular buyers — now five, including Sanders — and a part-time runner working for him.

"Sanders went on about getting [cannabis] across borders, asking me how it was done," Bleich later recalled. "There was lots of talk about wanting to set up a grow op — that was the main point of the meeting ... We agreed that 25 pounds would go to Day's shop in Newmarket and that we'd need the cash ... [Day's office] was in an industrial area, offices at front, garage space in back with a big door and construction tools."

Bleich said cannabis could be sold for $4,000 a pound in the U.S. and told Day and the undercover officer that the best way to smuggle cannabis across the border was inside the tire of a truck. But the cannabis had to be left a bit moist, Bleich explained, or it would be crushed to a powder.

Bleich also asked Sanders' help in getting a mortgage. Even though Bleich had $35,000 in savings, his legitimate income was too small for him to qualify for a normal mortgage and he wanted Sanders to help him find an "illegal banker" who would help Bleich buy a house.

At 9:08 p.m., Day and Bleich walked out of the Newmarket Keg and drove north — talking about the Barrie grow op, Bleich describing a spray to kill spider mites — until they pulled into the Barrie car-pool lot. Bleich got into his own pickup and drove home.

The next day, Bleich drove to Sunnidale Township, not far from Barrie, and stopped at the Clearview Self Storage. He briefly went into one of the storage units, then phoned Day. Bleich said he had "25 feet of rope" and told Day to tell Sanders to have the money ready. Bleich arrived at Day's place of business in Newmarket around 6:00 p.m., lifted two medium-sized cardboard boxes printed with the word *Rona* out of the cargo area of his truck and carried them through the back door.

Waiting inside were Day, Sanders and Constable Jones, who was pretending to be Sanders' runner. Bleich later described Jones as "shorter, five-eight, stocky, white hair, 35 or so." Bleich handed a box each to Day and Jones, then Bleich and Jones went into an office and closed the door. Jones counted the pounds and handed Bleich a paper bag from McDonald's with $37,500 in cash inside. After Bleich went home, the police examined the outdoor-grown cannabis. There were no fingerprints on any of the 25 shrink-wrapped bags.

Later, Bleich needed to resupply. He met DaSilva's runner, Yvan Guindon, in the lot of the Shell gas station on Yonge Street in Newmarket. Guindon lifted two heavy-looking black suitcases from the back of his pickup and put them into Bleich's pickup.

The OPP followed Guindon's Chevrolet Silverado from the Shell station to Highway 401 east. Guindon drove nonstop to Quebec. At the provincial border, the Quebec provincial police, Sûreté du Québec, took over the tail. In Hudson, Quebec, DaSilva's runner stopped to eat at "Woot!" Smokemeat & Pizza, then drove onto the ferry to Guindon's hometown, Oka, where contact was lost.

. . . .

In addition to those of Bleich, Day was insinuating himself into the business dealings of several other Canadian druglords. On January 27, 2010, at the Orchard Family Restaurant in Mississauga, Fred "Goggles" Freeman sat and talked to Day — and Day's hidden tape recorder — about his wish to "go legit," because his past convictions meant that if he was caught again, he would go to jail for a very long time. Perhaps the rest of his life.

Despite that wish, Freeman was deep into a new plan involving cannabis — to grow "under the umbrella of Health Canada." He would grow the plants legally, for ill people with a license to use cannabis as medicine. Freeman would model his business on the thriving cannabis market in California. He said that, of all the cannabis he grew, half would be sold legally as medicine and half would be sold "out the back door."

Freeman talked about a female friend who had a growing license and how he had helped her to set up her legal indoor grow op. He had also helped others to set up legal grow ops. He complained that many of these ill gardeners were "lazy, would forget to turn the lights on and lose half their plants."

Two days later, at the Husky Truck Stop at the intersection of Highway 400 and Highway 88, Day met again with Freeman, who had brought along a man called Chris. Heavyset and in his 40s, Chris was Freeman's associate in the Health Canada plan.

Day drove them both to Sudbury. Freeman carried a small bag of dried cannabis flowers and Chris had two film canisters full. During the four-hour drive trip on Highway 400, Freeman and Chris each smoked three joints. Near Barrie, they passed what remained of the Molson building and Day suggested they go back there for the new grow op.

Freeman laughed. "I thought they tore down that place."

Briefing

In 1928, Hamilton gangster Rocco Perri, who started with a grocery on Hamilton's Hess Street North and described himself to *Toronto Star* reporter Ernest Hemingway as "King of the Bootleggers," went to prison.

Perri's common-law wife, Bessie Starkman, took over his gang temporarily. She was the only Jewish woman to ever be a boss in an Italian crime syndicate. Starkman aggressively expanded the Hamilton gang's activities into the new markets of opium, cocaine and cannabis.

Starkman was shot dead in her garage in 1930; Perri disappeared.

For a long time after that, Hamilton was the headquarters for illegal drug trafficking in Ontario.

The Silence
of the Beavers

"I would just move to another site and start again."
—Drago Dolic

May 21, 2010.

The Federal Correctional Institution at Pollock, Louisiana, is 15 miles north of Alexandria and surrounded by Kisatchie National Forest — a beautiful wild preserve, full of old-growth pine and cypress forests, bogs, hummingbirds, cicadas and many crystal methamphetamine laboratories.

Glenn Day and his OPP drug-unit handlers had arranged for Day to visit Dolic's prison. Day had been banned from the U.S. ever since his conviction in Florida in 1997 for trafficking cannabis oil, but an exception was made for Project Birmingham. Day crossed the border and went to Louisiana to collect evidence from his boss and friend.

When Day arrived at Pollock, the front-lobby officer checked his identification and told Day to sign Form BP-224, declaring that he was not carrying anything that was a security threat and would agree to a personal search. (Day was not wearing the tape recorder; this part of Project Birmingham would rely on his memory and honesty.)

Day was subjected to a metal detector, random pat-downs and an ion spectrometer machine, which — a visitor's guide explained — could detect tiny particles of "narcotics or marijuana."

Day and Dolic met in a room shared with other federal inmates and their visitors. Dolic, like the other inmates, wore a khaki-colored, collarless jumpsuit and prison boots. The two men were allowed to shake hands once at the start of the visit and once at the end, and Dolic had to stay seated the entire time. Day was allowed to buy sandwiches for Dolic during the visit — sandwiches that Dolic would give to other prisoners, as a way of boosting his social status. Day bought more and more, eventually spending $30 on sandwiches for various mooching convicts.

Dolic started the conversation by talking about his family. Just before the RCMP had seized his house in Mississauga, he said, his wife had taken out $300,000 from a second mortgage on it, which she used to buy another house in Mississauga for half a million. He explained that the monthly mortgage payments were $2,500, plus $500 in other expenses. Robert Bleich was giving one of Dolic's relatives $3,000 to $10,000 a month.

Day talked about his visit to the old Molson plant and his chat with Larry McGee. Dolic commented on the wiring work McGee had done at a grow op, saying that McGee was "real good" at setting up bypasses to steal electricity. He recommended that Day use McGee as an electrician.

The next day, Day visited again. Among other topics, Dolic talked about "The Deaf Guy" (Bob DeRosa), explaining how Freeman had introduced Dolic to him. He complained that DeRosa had squeezed him for huge rent increases once the grow ops at Molson and Oro were running. In spite of his complaints, Dolic said that DeRosa might be able to help find a place for a new grow op.

Dolic also discussed his partnership with Robert Bleich. They had had some bad luck recently — $36,000 in cash had been accidentally sent to the wrong address and confiscated by police, who then approached Dolic's mother-in-law and asked her questions about the money. Dolic and Bleich had also lost another $87,000 when their runner was stopped and searched by police.

Despite these setbacks, Dolic was eager to expand his prison-run drug empire with Day's help. He tried to interest Day in an outdoor growing scheme with Bleich, using a strain of cannabis called Ice. Not to be confused with crystal methamphetamine, also known as "ice," this cannabis is a 50-50 indica-sativa hybrid bred in Holland in the 1990s and the winner of *High Times* magazine's Cannabis Cup in 1998. Ice is known for rapid growth, large clusters of flowers, a high THC level and a harsh, hash-like taste.

Dolic suggested growing Ice in cornfields — Day should get some knee-high clones, take them 10 to 20 rows into a cornfield and plant a row of the babies about 33 yards long, remove some cornstalks so the babies get more sunlight and sprinkle pellets of time-release fertilizer around the base of the plants. There should be no reason to return until the crop is ready.

Dolic told Day that if he grew a single Ice plant in his backyard, when it was ready, that would indicate that its sisters in the cornfield were ready too. Dolic estimated that Day could expect to harvest a pound of dried flower per outdoor plant (a yield less than half that of some indoor grow ops).

They also talked about growing an outdoor cannabis strain called Blueberry, which Dolic said Bleich would be able to supply. Blueberry was another sativa-indica hybrid, bred in California in the 1980s from a strain called Juicy Fruit. The strain's name came from the cool blue tint to the plant and its flowers, as well as the smoke's "very fruity" flavour. It was designed to be grown outdoors, with organic fertilizers. Blueberry's effect on the human brain has been described as "pleasantly euphoric," with a tendency to cause short-term amnesia. It won first place in its category in the 2000 *High Times* Cannabis Cup, and also at a cannabis contest sponsored by Canadian cannabis-rights leader Marc Emery (before Emery's 2010 extradition to the U.S. on seed-trafficking charges).

The two men also discussed codes to use when talking about drugs in emails.

On their third and last visit the next day, Dolic immediately started talking about the cornfield scheme. Day changed the conversation to indoor grow ops, asking for advice on how to set one up. Dolic said, "Go see The Deaf Guy" about a rental property, and added that if Bob DeRosa agreed at the beginning that the monthly lease would be $10,000 and that electricity would be $4,000, Day should expect to eventually pay double or triple that. Day should be able to set up 100 candles for $100,000. Dolic recommended DaSilva as an electrician, saying that "The Frenchman" was "good and clean." He said DeRosa might have some grow lights Day could use and that Bleich could help Day sell the product. Pelikan would manage the trimmers.

Dolic would email Bleich, asking him to help Day. Millions of dollars in profit would be made in a few years, Dolic predicted.

Day asked Dolic if he had ever thought about what would happen if the Barrie grow op was raided by the police.

"Yeah," Dolic answered, "I would just move to another site and start again."

Again, Dolic accused Tripper of telling the police about the Barrie grow op. Day listened and remembered. As he was about to leave the room, Dolic said, "Don't be a follower! Be a leader!"

. . . .

A few months later, in the winter of 2010, Hamilton police officers with search warrants raided two grow ops in industrial buildings. The first was a building at 25 Sawyer Street, where they arrested one man. Later, police officers swarmed into a building at 1212 Leaside Road; nobody was found there.

Both of the properties had been strongly secured, with heavy steel doors, guard dogs, barbed-wire fencing and video cameras.

Police seized almost 5,000 plants at the two properties — a haul worth $4.25 million, according to authorities.

At the Leaside Road grow op, police also found nine pounds of dried cannabis flowers (worth $20,000) and over 50 grams of cannabis oil (worth $1,250).

And who was behind these grow ops?

Police identified the man they'd arrested on Sawyer Street as Robin Summerhayes — the member of Dolic's gang who, in 1997, had gone with Glenn Day to Miami to buy cannabis oil. Like Day, Summerhayes had received a long U.S. prison sentence for that, and had served the last part of it in Canada.

Summerhayes, 49, had a high school education and now worked in construction. In addition to the Florida conviction, he had twice been convicted of drug offences in Canada; he had been fined $100 in 1984 — when he was 23 — for "simple possession" and, that same year, he had been jailed for 90 days for trafficking in hash. Now he, his wife and the youngest of his three daughters lived on a 10-acre horse farm near Guelph, Ontario. The couple had two grandchildren, with a third on the way.

Police seized the $3,010 that Summerhayes had been carrying at the time of his arrest. When they searched his home, they found — in his middle dresser drawer — three small ziplock bags of hash and one of dried cannabis flowers.

Was Day the informant who tipped Hamilton police to the two grow ops?

Probably.

Summerhayes was sentenced to two years. The Ontario Society for the Prevention of Cruelty to Animals seized the frightening dogs that had guarded both grow ops. The dogs, like their master, were caged.

. . . .

In June 2010, Bleich got an email from Dolic, who said it was okay to work with Glenn Day.

Despite that recommendation, Bleich later said he'd been getting "a bad vibe from Glenn and his buddy [Constable Sanders], who kept wanting more. They called many times over months. I didn't return some of the calls or I'd claim to be busy. Day would say, 'My buddy is up in Collingwood, give him a call.' But I never did. Day kept calling me, being a pest, every few weeks . . . Day was always whining that his construction business was in shit, he needed extra money. Me, I'm saying, 'I'll help you out.' . . . He wanted to meet with [DaSilva], so I met him again" — at the Cardinal Golf Course, just west of Newmarket. Bleich later said that Day "was good at golf, he likes to play . . . He doesn't cheat."

At the golf course, Day talked about his visit with Dolic, and Bleich asked how Day, with his criminal record, had managed to get across the border. Day said he just filled in the form and was approved.

Bleich mentioned that he had just received a recent photograph of Dolic, sent to Bleich by Dolic's sponsor at Alcoholics Anonymous.

As they played golf, they discussed business. Day asked a lot of questions. Bleich complained that he was selling only 50 to 60 pounds of cannabis a month, while sending up to $10,000 monthly to one of Dolic's relatives, plus $500 monthly directly to Dolic. He said he was not growing an outdoor crop this year; it was too much work. He preferred to just buy his cannabis from Jeff DaSilva.

Day said he wanted to buy 300 babies and asked Bleich to set up a meeting with DaSilva. Bleich said that he would, for sometime the following week. Since DaSilva owed Dolic money, Bleich suggested DaSilva could be paid for his work by a reduction of that debt.

Day asked for DaSilva's phone number. Bleich said no.

During the prison visit, Day explained, Dolic had told Day how to divide the profits from the new grow op. Now Day explained it to Bleich — they would all be partners, with Day getting 37 percent, Bleich and Dolic sharing a further 37 percent, Hould getting 25 percent as the main guy on-site and somebody with no criminal record to sign the lease, getting 5 percent as the fall guy.

After the golf game, Bleich and Day went their separate ways.

Bleich phoned DaSilva and, as he later described, "I said buddy [Day] had a couple hundred thousand to put up front for a grow op. Then [DaSilva] said he could come. I was to set up a meeting in Kingston."

Late in the afternoon, Bleich phoned Day, saying he had spoken with Jeff DaSilva and that the meeting would be in Kingston next Monday. Bleich told Day to bring his golf clubs.

· · · · · · ·

A few days later, Glenn Day went to Bob DeRosa's farmhouse in Phelpston. Nobody was home, so Day left a business card. When he did not hear anything for a few days, he and his hidden tape recorder went back. This time, DeRosa was home.

Day said he had learned the address from Larry McGee. DeRosa said that McGee "is no fucking good! He's a rat!" He was furious, and told Day a story — which his brother Vincent would later deny — about how McGee had found a gun belonging to Bob at the Molson grow op and had told Vincent about it, infuriating Bob.

DeRosa explained that McGee had had a little grow op of his own in an area of the Molson building that only he had access to, yet he was never charged by the police, and that McGee had gone frequently to the police station for interviews. DeRosa got more and more angry, spewing his wrongheaded idea that McGee had been a police informant. Ingratitude! After all, Bob DeRosa ranted, he was the one who had taken McGee "off the streets of St. Catharines" and given the guy a job!

DeRosa mentioned again that he had a gun collection and called McGee "a rat piece of shit," adding threateningly, "It won't be long now." He said he would put McGee into the trunk of a car "like a dog and beat him until he is dead!"

Day told DeRosa that the reason he was here was that he had visited Dolic in prison, and Dolic had suggested contacting DeRosa about a location for a new grow op. DeRosa said that he had heard about Dolic's 27-year sentence. How many lights would Day need, Bob DeRosa asked.

"Thirty to 50."

DeRosa said Day would need an industrial location. Barrie was no good, because the upcoming G8 summit would attract a lot of police. Day suggested a spot near an airport, to evade police helicopters. DeRosa assured Day that he could find a good place within a week.

DeRosa also claimed, falsely, that he had a relative who worked for the Ontario Provincial Police and gave him inside information. He said this relative had warned him before the Molson raid and that this warning was how some of the workers had escaped arrest.

Switching the conversation to sales, DeRosa asked if Day could sell cannabis for less than $2,000 a pound. He wanted two pounds at first, as a tester, and 10 to 20 pounds a week after that. (Bob DeRosa's license to legally possess medical cannabis was limited to a quarter of a pound.) He told Day that if he bought it at $1,950, he would sell it for $2,000, making a profit of $50 per pound.

"I'm not greedy, but it would be nice to make some money," DeRosa said.

Day explained that he was going to see his supplier on Monday and would let DeRosa know. They exchanged phone numbers. Once Day had "the weed," they would meet here, at the bison farm.

. . . .

The next day, Day got a text from Bleich about buying the babies from DaSilva. The meeting in Kingston on Monday would be for lunch only, Bleich texted, because DaSilva had no time for golf.

In the morning, Day and Bleich met for breakfast at the Husky Truck Stop at highways 400 and 88, then got into Day's black GMC pickup truck. As they drove, Bleich asked, "So how are you going to explain it to [DaSilva]?"

"Tell him we got a hundred grand," Day said. Later, Day asked, "What do you think — we're going to go with [legal] hydro or we're going to [illegally] bypass?"

Bleich said it "would be nice to bypass."

"No kidding," Day said. "We could save a lot of money."

"How you bypass," Bleich said, "all that, I don't know how all that works." Later, he told Day about a fishing trip he'd made to Lake Nipissing, and they talked about losing weight, exercise and various outdoor activities. When the subject of Fred Freeman came up, Bleich said, "He's dying to get [a drug deal] going . . . [He] kept calling, calling, calling. I just want nothing to do with him."

"Well, he fucked you over," Day said.

"Yeah, yeah, that too. But I just don't want nothing to do with him, you know? Fuck, it's the Chinaman [Freeman's new business associate]. I don't trust him anyways."

"Who, the Chinaman?"

Bleich said, "Yeah . . . I got a six year old . . . and I got a whole life going and I don't need no fucking extra headaches that I don't already have . . . Fuck them, eh. Fuck. Whatever . . . I make five grand a month so I can cover my fucking bills . . . and I fucking, you know, get to go out for dinner once every couple of weeks or once every week with my old lady and my kid and I'm happy."

In Kingston, Day stopped in a parking lot, where he and Bleich met Jeff DaSilva, who had driven from near Montreal in his big purple GMC pickup. DaSilva stood by Day's truck.

Bleich said, "You going to get in here or what? . . . Okay, let him in."

Unlocking the doors, Day laughingly said to DaSilva, "*Bon. Oui.* You motherfucker."

"It's not as clean as it used to be, fucker," DaSilva complained as he got into Day's truck, and he gave Day directions to The Keg.

"I thought The Keg was over where it says you get off the fucking highway," Bleich said.

"No, it's all crap there," DaSilva said.

It turned out The Keg was closed — it was between lunchtime and dinnertime — so they ended up at the Raging Bull on Ontario Street. They sat at an outdoor patio table and ordered shrimp cocktails. Bleich and DaSilva ordered wine, and Day, who said he was off alcohol, ordered a glass of pop.

Before the talk began, Day saw Bleich slip some money into DaSilva's hand — earlier Bleich had mentioned to Day that he was carrying $30,000. DaSilva asked Day about Dolic: "So how's he doing?"

"Well, he's doing all right," Day said. "Well, he told me to come see you, so that's why we're here."

"First of all, I'd like to have another big [grow op]," Bleich said.

Day said, "We're trying to do something — uh, you know, I got enough for 40 lights."

"I'm just more interested in points [percentage of ownership] now than I am in building," DaSilva said. ". . . Because for me it's a way I'll be able to keep going to the [motocross] races and, you know, having fun with my family."

"Yeah," Bleich said.

"I wanted buildings a while ago," DaSilva continued. "Now I want to make sure I build again next year and the year after and the year after . . . It's tougher than it used to be."

"It's not much to set up 40 candles," Bleich said.

"At least 60 to 70 thousand," DaSilva said. "It's not much more to set up 80 lights."

Day said that his associate would put in $100,000 to get it built. "What'd yours cost?" he asked. "Like, what was your —"

DaSilva interrupted: "Which one?"

"In Oro," Day said.

"In Oro, my whole bill . . . I got that whole thing done for 200 [thousand dollars]."

Bleich jumped in. "Yeah and he had 60 lights in for, like, 70, 80 grand."

"It used to be 1,000 bucks a light and now it's more like 2,000," DaSilva said.

"Ours worked out for 333 a light at Molson," Bleich said.

"To build," said DaSilva.

"To build, yeah. We were $990,000 or something from the time it was we were paying workers and the time you [DaSilva] came in and the time we bought everything . . . Everything right to the first chemicals, dirt, everything. Babies . . . 300 lights [to start]."

DaSilva mentioned that he had an indoor grow op now with 48 lights, producing two pounds a light and with a crop due for harvest at the end of the month. He said he had a long-term business partner.

The conversation moved on and DaSilva said it would be nice if Bleich could start selling more of DaSilva's cannabis. Bleich agreed that he would try to sell more.

Day asked DaSilva about buying 300 babies for a friend of Dolic's. DaSilva said that for a friend of Dolic's, he would see about paying for them himself. His runner would drive to Barrie next week and deliver the 300 babies to Day and 10 to 20 pounds of cannabis for Bleich. If by next week Day had found a location for a grow op, DaSilva would go with his runner to Barrie so he could take a look at the place; if no location had been found by next week, the runner would go to Barrie alone.

The three men also discussed new growing methods. DaSilva had learned how to spray the walls of a grow op to cut the smell so much that the air did not have to be pumped outside. "There's no more exhausts . . . It's well worth it to not have an exhaust problem in the winter." DaSilva mentioned that he still had the same spray gun he had used at the Molson grow op. He spoke of using powdered plant food, as opposed to old-fashioned liquid fertilizer. He also described a new machine that could do most of the trimming: "It's like, put [the cannabis] in . . . take it out when it's ready . . . It's sick! sick! sick! sick! sick! sick! . . . how many less people you can use."

DaSilva mentioned that he also had a crop of outdoor cannabis — the Miracle strain — that would be ready for harvest at the end of the month. Bleich asked how much he was pulling in, and DaSilva said he was making $48,000 for each outdoor harvest.

They agreed that as soon as the new grow op — now planned to have 80 candles, burning on stolen electricity — was up and running, they would start building another one.

Bleich said it was important that their cannabis not resemble "Chinese weed," which "people are getting sick of . . . It's trimmed different, it looks different . . . it smells different . . . it's just shit. Fuck, you don't even get high enough . . . Well, you get high, right, but it's just — it's your 20-minute buzz, right. You don't get no, hmm . . . [Customers] are looking for the kick."

Rather than the despicable "Chinese weed," Bleich recommended growing Blueberry and "the skunk." Regarding skunkweed, DaSilva said, "not many people are doing it cause it stinks so much."

"That's why they like it," Bleich countered.

They talked about how annoying it was when potential customers opened several vacuum-pack bags to sample the product and then didn't buy anything. "Fuck," Bleich said, "he'll open up 15, 20 of them on you. You're getting dirty, all of a sudden you've opened up half and then they go, 'Oh, I don't want none' or 'I'll take one.'"

Without using the word *cocaine*, Day asked DaSilva if he was involved in that product. "No, no, never, never, never," DaSilva said, "never since I got off. Never, never even touch it."

Day agreed: "Once you start playing with that shit . . . Don't ever get involved in that shit."

Conversation progressed to someone they knew who had recently retired from the drug trade.

Bleich said, "He's just growing strawberries and blueberries or something. He's pretty much done. He's done . . . Everyone I know is old."

"Getting young blood without risk is almost impossible," DaSilva said.

They decided to hire middle-aged Denis Hould to run the day-to-day gardening operations.

And then they discussed some practicalities of the operation. Bleich said, "We just gotta think about water going down the drain

. . . That was a big thing at Molson's too. That was a lot of water there."

"Well, look at what happened at St. Catharines [Ssonix]," Day said.

And later, Day asked DaSilva, "You got that shit coming? . . . The babies?"

"Buy the babies," Bleich said.

"Yeah," said DaSilva, "I'll get them next week. Middle of next week."

When the subject of Fred Freeman came up again, Bleich complained that after he, Bleich, went to prison, Freeman "didn't call or text or ask or send a message with somebody or give [money] to my old lady. Dan [Dolic] did right. That's Dan's nature . . . [Freeman] didn't do nothing. I was his fucking runner for like 17 years . . . Since I was 14 I bent over backwards for that guy. For nothing. I went and seen him a couple of times [in Vancouver] after I got out, that was it."

"I heard he's broke anyways," Day said. "Fuck him."

"Yeah, yeah," Bleich said. "He owes my one buddy 600 bucks for a QP [quarter pound] . . . [My buddy] hasn't seen him in like over a month."

"QP for personal?" DaSilva asked.

"Yeah."

"And he's not paying for it?"

"Yeah."

"Well, it's not a good sign," DaSilva said.

"No," said Bleich, "he's not doing good."

"Not him but his buddy, the Chinaman," DaSilva said.

"Yeah."

Bleich said that Freeman "is a fucking slimy sneaker, that's what. Dan was pissed off at him too. Fucking Fred was doing Ritalin and fucking selling lots of those and bringing it in from out west and didn't give Dan a penny . . . [Freeman] was coming out to his house once a week. [Dan] started just saying he wasn't there. He wouldn't answer the door."

DaSilva laughed.

Bleich continued: "Cocksucker. And he was working with someone else out there too, another one of our friends. You know, didn't give Dan a fucking penny, just worked behind the fucking door."

Day asked, "Did Dan give him . . . part of that fucking Molsons . . . because he fucking introduced him to Bob [DeRosa]?"

Nobody answered Day's police-inspired question.

"That guy lost me and he's lost key people," Bleich continued about Freeman. "Most of his fucking people that we used to sell to, they love me more than they love him. I just don't bother going down [to Niagara Falls] to go see them. I'd go down there in a heartbeat but, fuck, they'd be all over me like shits on a fly." Bleich laughed.

Discussion shifted to electricity for the proposed new grow op. Bleich asked, "Are we going to pay for it or steal it?"

"Steal it," DaSilva said.

Bleich later said that, at this time, he "wanted no part of [operating] a new grow op." He was still on parole and was just hoping for a finder's fee. Bleich told Day and DaSilva, "I don't want to grow it, but — I just — I'll sell it."

After lunch, DaSilva asked Bleich how much money Bleich had surreptitiously handed him at the start of the meeting. Bleich said he didn't know exactly — it was either $24,000 or $26,000 and that he still owed DaSilva $9,000.

The three men walked out of the Raging Bull and stood near DaSilva's truck, talking about different ways to divide up the profits and how to handle Bob DeRosa. Bleich said that after making $3 or $4 million from the new grow op, he'd consider retirement.

He and Day went to Day's car and drove back west to the Husky. DaSilva, however, was followed by the OPP to a gas station. The purple GMC truck then led the OPP team at high speed to the 401 eastbound. At the provincial border, surveillance was taken over by Sûreté du Québec, which lost contact with the speeding vehicle near Highway 116 and Autoroute 30 in Longueuil. But the government knew where DaSilva lived. They staked out his home. At 7:17 p.m., DaSilva's purple truck arrived at his home in a suburb of Montreal, Saint Jean-sur-Richelieu.

The following week, Bleich phoned Day and said "the job was done," meaning he had picked up the 300 babies from DaSilva. They arranged to meet at the same Husky Truck Stop, but Bleich later phoned back and said he now wanted to meet at the liquor store in Angus, Ontario.

When Bleich arrived at the Angus LCBO, he parked beside Day. He took four sealed cardboard boxes from the back of his Toyota Tundra and put them into the trunk of Day's car.

Bleich told Day to "make sure to put some water on them."

When Bleich left, police opened the boxes. In each were a tray and 75 babies.

Briefing

The drug trade and the gun trade are linked.

Most illegal guns in Canada are smuggled from the United States. Tens of thousands of U.S. firearms are seized by Canadian police every year. In 2012, Toronto ex-mayor David Miller called it "a river of guns flowing north."

Drug dealers desire guns to protect their property from predatory outlaws, enforce contracts, resolve disagreements, eliminate competition, harm informants, intimidate the general public and deter police officers.

Some in the drug trade want guns for emotional reasons: to boost their sense of power, belonging and manhood.

Narcs Listening to B101 and The Edge

"Have to pay trimmers, pay people, pay the babies, pay the earth, keep paying other stuff and then another rent's going to hit us and then before we know it, fuck, we're fucked."
— Jeff DaSilva

Glenn Day and Constable Jones, who was posing as Day's runner, went to a potential grow-op site at an industrial building in Welland, near the canal and right behind a Canadian Tire, to meet Bob DeRosa.

They waited outside until a black Jeep pulled up. DeRosa was inside, with two other men he introduced as the managers of the property, one of whom he said he had known for 10 years. Day openly told the two property managers he'd just met that he wanted the place for "growing weed."

They looked around inside the building, where people were busy working, and Day and Jones took photos. DeRosa suggested that Day set up a scrap-metal recycling company as a front. He also said he would like a cut of the grow op's profit, "just a little bit."

The property managers said it would cost between $9,000 and $10,000 to rent the place, with first and last month's rent paid in advance. Day and Jones examined the building's power supply.

They walked up to the second floor, but DeRosa stayed downstairs because of his bad back. Day said the second floor would be good for the living and sleeping areas for the workers. The men went back downstairs and discussed renovations.

Day then asked the property managers when he could take possession and was told the place would be empty in a week or two. Day said he needed a place for the end of the month, adding that Jones would be the one to sign any lease.

Bob DeRosa said he had another place to show Day in downtown Hamilton, but needed a few more days to set up a time to view it.

When the meeting ended, DeRosa and the property managers drove away in the Jeep. OPP officers followed them to a Tim Hortons on Lundy's Lane in Niagara Falls, where DeRosa got out of the black Jeep and into a blue Jeep registered to his wife. One of the property managers got into a gray Mercedes, and the three carpoolers drove off in their separate vehicles.

Shortly afterwards, Bob DeRosa flew to Panama — by way of Camagüey, Cuba — and then back, stopping again in Camagüey.

. . . .

Glenn Day, after a long day's work reshingling some houses in Barrie, was told by his OPP handlers to visit the Phelpston farm again. During the drive, he listened to Barrie radio station B101. As he approached the Phelpston farm, the radio in Day's truck was blasting Ke$ha's pop hit "Your Love Is My Drug."

At the door to the farmhouse, Bob DeRosa invited Day in. Day went to the bathroom to urinate — the tinkling sound of his stream recorded by the OPP body pack under his clothes. Without washing his hands, Day left the bathroom and was introduced to DeRosa's family. Bob offered Day some chicken his wife had cooked for dinner.

During small talk, Day was very polite, at one point saying, "I just want to make everybody happy, you know?"

Later, talking about business, Day told DeRosa that DaSilva was coming to look at the Welland property the next day; DeRosa said he could not make the meeting — he had a doctor's appointment for his back that he had been waiting three months for and could not miss.

Following the orders of his OPP handler, Day asked DeRosa if he could supply firearms. Day wanted two Glocks for "the Kid" (Constable Jones). DeRosa said he would talk to an associate and "get two Glocks" next week.

Day said, "Are the serial numbers off?"

"What?"

"Are the serial numbers off?"

"Yeah, I'll take them off. I'll go see buddy Wednesday or Thursday. See what he's got on hand. Let you know."

On the subject of a new grow op, Bob DeRosa said, "I'll get you good spots, I'll get you protection, I'll get you whatever the fuck you need!" He even offered to provide special air-conditioning units. He next mentioned a potential grow-op location in Hamilton that he had been working on: a three-story building near City Hall downtown.

DeRosa switched topics and asked Day the current selling price for cocaine.

"I heard they are a lot of money — 60 [thousand dollars a kilogram]," Day said.

"Fuck, they are expensive right now," DeRosa replied. "Fuck, I heard Niagara [was] 44. I thought that was too high. I don't mind paying 40. . . . But untouched, eh?" (*Untouched* meant not diluted or cut.)

"Yeah, untouched for sure," Day said.

Later, Day told a story: "I was trying to get . . . hash right from India and I backed out because they had that fucking bombing over there and they were checking fucking little handbags, they were checking people, they were stopping people in the street and saying, 'Let me look in your bag.' In Bombay."

Bob DeRosa said, "How much?"

"Five hundred dollars."

"For a kilo?"

"Yeah."

"Pure? Pure?"

Day said, about smuggling hash from India to Canada, "[My hash connection] done it five times. Him and Dan [Dolic] . . . used to do it all the time." He described smuggling the hash into Montreal, then transporting it to Toronto and Newmarket in CN trains.

"What's the problem?" DeRosa asked.

"He's scared now because when it comes from the mountains and they gotta walk into the city and they're checking all the bags because of the bombings."

Bob DeRosa said he had just returned from Panama and Cuba, and had plans to go back to Panama in 10 days to arrange the shipment of a container to Halifax with 200 kilos of cocaine. He called the members of the cartel "good people," mentioning that one of them had recently died in a Mexican prison. He was in contact with a cartel member who was a student in Calgary. He told Day that the 200-kilo shipment would be followed by a one-ton shipment, and invited Day to get involved in the scheme.

Discussing the risks of drug trafficking, Day said, "That's a lot of time [in prison] for that shit if you get caught, a lot of time for that shit."

"I know," DeRosa said. "Get caught, it's 25, 30 [years.] You don't come out. That's it. Done. A chance you take, but I'm getting old."

Day said, "Look at Dan [Dolic] — 30 years."

"He's going to be lucky to get out," DeRosa said. "If his health is good, he comes out alive."

"He won't," Day said. "He's 50 now."

"He's that old?"

"Well, I'm 48," Day said.

"I'm 52."

Day said, "He's 50 . . . He's got at least another 22 years, if he gets some time off. That's 75 fucking years old . . . He's not doing nothing [for exercise]. Nothing. He's still big, he hasn't lost a fucking ounce."

"Why doesn't he work out?" asked DeRosa. (Both Day and Bob DeRosa were obese themselves.)

"I don't know. When I [was in a U.S. prison for cannabis-oil importation], I hung with Tommy Gambino [a high-level New York ganster and son of the founder of the Gambino Mafia syndicate] . . . I was with Tommy. You know, the old man? . . . I was in Pennsylvania with him."

"You were with him?" DeRosa sounded impressed.

"Yeah."

"Minimum [security prison]?"

"Yeah. Well, it was medium."

"Medium-minimum."

"I was with a bunch of captains from different Families," Day boasted. ". . . I hung with a bunch of guys from Sicily."

"Sicily."

"Yeah. They're good guys."

Sounding very impressed, DeRosa said, "Fuck."

Later, at a mention of Larry McGee, DeRosa started ranting again about the meek-looking, blond-haired maintenance man who had once punched him in the mouth: "I'm telling you and I'll go tell him to his face, it means that he's going to get it! It's just a matter of time. I tell you, he's going to get it, so read the papers . . . I'm fucking telling you, read the papers. The reason why I haven't killed him yet is because I don't want to spend a dollar on legal fees and I don't want to do a day of time. He's going to fucking get it. So I'm telling you, let me see, I've got a few favors [owed to me by the Santa Marta cocaine cartel]. This deal goes through, they'll come in here for a fucking holiday for a week, fly in to do the fucking job [kill McGee], fly back out. As a favor. Not paying, no. Not even talking. And whoever is there with him [gets killed too]." DeRosa paused, then said, "I'm telling you, that's how fucked I am in a rage. As soon as his fucking name comes up, my hair starts to go straight in a rage."

He sighed and said, "But anyways," and changed the subject.

As Day drove away, B101 on the pickup's radio blasted "Break Your Heart" by Ludacris and Eminem's "Love the Way You Lie."

. . . .

At another meeting with Bob DeRosa at the Phelpston farmhouse, Day asked about Bob's bad back.

"Terrible. Fuck," said Day's host.

"What did the doctor say?"

"My spine is going. Got to put me on fucking methadone, oxy — three or four options. I can't take injections, because my spine is too sensitive. It's degenerated, you know? A fucking disease that narrows your spine . . . I tell you, I'm fighting it . . . I don't even smoke pot. I don't do anything. Maybe have a couple of glasses of wine. Sometimes a couple shots of vodka. With people over, you know."

Later, moving to business talk, DeRosa ranted about how he preferred working with Chinese people on drug deals because "the Italians are too fucking greedy." And about his guns, he said, "I got restricted and unrestricted [firearms] legally . . . I'm clean . . . I got a Glock here that's bigger than a Glock. Mine's bigger, mine is the same size as the American police use — one size bigger than the police here." He said the guns came with "two clips."

"Two clips per gun?" Day asked.

"Yeah."

"Okay."

"I always — I always ask for two."

DeRosa spoke excitedly about the potential profit in this firearms deal: he'd buy the two guns on the Six Nations reserve for $3,500 each and sell them to Day for $4,000 each. Day could then sell the handguns to someone else for a higher price. "Makes us some fast money, man, right away," DeRosa enthused.

Later in the meeting, he asked Day, "You know where I can get some tranquilizer for cats?"

"For what?"

"Tranquilizer."

"For —"

"From veterinarians. It's called ketamine . . . You know where I can get any of that? A friend of mine needs a fucking favor. I guess they use that shit to party . . . Have you ever dealt in that?"

Day said, "Never, ever."

The conversation then turned to Larry McGee again. DeRosa complained to the highly paid police informant about the money he (incorrectly) imagined McGee had been paid as a police informant.

Day said, "Just be careful. Don't draw the heat . . . We don't need no heat."

"I'm not stupid . . . Hey, listen to me. If I had a muffler right now, I would have wasted him a long time ago. You know what a muffler is?"

"No."

DeRosa put his fingers in the shape of a gun, saying, "Okay, it goes on the end of these."

"Oh yeah, oh, oh, oh, oh yeah, yeah," Day nervously babbled. "Silencers."

DeRosa said that, after being interviewed so much by the police, McGee had been "shitting bricks, you understand what I'm saying. He knows because I told him. I said, 'Listen, buddy, I'm going to waste you.' I told him right to his fucking face, 'I'm going to waste you because you're going to wish you never fucking — you — You double cross me, I'm going to take your life!' — right to his face. He went fucking all shades." He added that, when he went to kill McGee, "Whoever's there — whoever's there — you know, a girlfriend, her kid, it doesn't matter. I'm going to fucking waste them while [McGee watches]. It's messier. You know what he did . . . I don't play games. You try to call my fucking bluff, you got some piece of fucking shit."

Later, more calmly, DeRosa talked about how his doctor had signed a form for medicinal cannabis. There were great prices and great selection at the Cannabis As Living Medicine compassion club on Queen Street East in Toronto. "They've even got fucking cookies!"

he raved. He said about his club, "They just got grabbed [by police], eh. Remember in the paper, maybe three, four weeks ago?"

"No."

"That was their place. But they dropped all the charges on the patients. The president, the owner — he's the only one up on charges. They're going to drop those too. It's compassion . . . nobody wants to touch them . . . You can't go in there and handcuff a fucking patient!"

He said he wanted to open his own compassion club. One had just opened up in Barrie, so the local market was covered, but he mentioned other possible locations in Ontario, including Hamilton. DeRosa urged Day to get involved in starting a compassion club somewhere, saying, "Keep it in mind . . . this is almost legitimate."

. . . .

On July 13, 2010, at 5:10 a.m., Jeff DaSilva was under surveillance by the Sûreté du Québec when he left his home in Saint Jean-sur-Richelieu, driving his purple Chevrolet pickup. He headed to the Flying J truck centre, where he met Yvan Guindon, who got into DaSilva's truck and took the wheel. Guindon drove from Quebec to the Jack Astor's restaurant in Burlington, where they met Glenn Day. DaSilva introduced Guindon, his runner, to Day as "the Old Man" (a nickname previously applied to Michael DiCicco). Guindon was sent off to take DaSilva's truck to a car wash, while DaSilva got into Day's vehicle. Day drove the Quebecois electrician to Welland.

"I'm starting to get tired, you know what I mean," DaSilva said.

"I hear you, bro," said Day.

"Plus I lost the tall guy [Bleich], so I have no main employee," DaSilva complained. ". . . He quit again."

"That fucking guy, always quitting. He fucking quit how many times with Dan?"

"He quit at least four times . . . He doesn't want to do the job . . . Well, yeah, fuck off."

As they drove, DaSilva talked about problems in his marriage and his need to spend more time with his wife, while Day spoke rudely about Dolic's wife, accusing her of various misdeeds.

DaSilva asked how Day, with his criminal record, was able to cross the border to visit Dolic in Louisiana. Day replied that, because he was Native, his status card enabled him to travel across the border at will.

Their conversation was so interesting that Day missed the exit to Welland. They had to get off the highway and turn the black pickup around.

"Hey," Day said, "are you able to get babies?"

"Yeah, yeah, yeah . . . I got a few guys," DaSilva said.

"Do you know who was supplying the odd babies at the Molson plant?"

"Somebody's doing babies there now?"

"No — do you know who used to supply them?"

"Uh, nope . . ."

"I figured you know . . . where to get the babies," Day said.

"Yeah," DaSilva replied, "but it's all [M39], that's all they're fucking doing and [Bleich] doesn't want 39 [which Bleich called "Chinese weed"] . . . I got two really good guys, but all they're doing is Royal 39 and regular 39."

As they toured the industrial building Bob DeRosa had located, they discussed various difficulties at previous big grow ops.

"Water was an issue at both places," DaSilva said. ". . . Both the one I built at St. Catharines [Ssonix] and the one, uh, up there."

"Yeah, up at Oro," Day said.

"Oro was an issue with water, that's for sure."

Day laughed.

"The hole didn't work, did it?" DaSilva said.

Day laughed so hard that he choked, gasping, "Fuck! Holy fuck!"

The conversation moved to the Molson grow up. DaSilva asked Day not to say the word *Molson* — because "they can still fucking arrest me for that shit" — and to call it the "funny farm" instead.

After a technical discussion of electricity theft, Day said, "How come you never ever fucking did something else with your knowledge?"

"Sometimes I wonder," DaSilva said, "because I would have made just as much money in any other business . . . Nobody else can do what I can do . . . [It] doesn't really matter. You know why, though. In Quebec there's so much fucking stupid rules . . . I have to do the test, I have to do the exam."

DaSilva stressed how important it was to make sure that the grow op made business sense. If the rent was too high, he said, "we'll have almost nothing left once we're done. Have to pay trimmers, pay people, pay the babies, pay the earth, keep paying other stuff and then another rent's going to hit us and then before we know it, fuck, we're fucked."

Day said that if DaSilva did not like the Welland building, Bob DeRosa had arranged an industrial site in Hamilton, near City Hall. DaSilva thought the Welland building's rent was too high, plus the building needed to be connected to the 600 volt electrical service. To build a grow op here, DaSilva said, $100,000 would not be enough; $175,000 was more like it.

The two men decided to get disposable cell phones and adopt new nicknames: DaSilva would be "Pepper," Day would be "Tomahawk" and Bleich would be "Legs."

DaSilva said he was in a hurry to get back to Quebec to "pick up some babies." He added that he was supposed to meet with Bleich later that day to pick up $40,000, but Bleich did not have the cash ready, so he or his runner would return to Ontario in a few days. DaSilva complained about communications with Bleich, saying, "He's hard to get in touch with. I can spend four days beeping him." So they agreed to cut Bleich out of their business plans and deal directly together.

DaSilva asked about the 300 babies Day had bought, and Day said he had given them to a buddy, who had planted them.

After the meeting, the men were driving back through Welland.

They passed a roadside sign that attracted DaSilva's attention. "What's that?" he exclaimed. "'*Delilah's Massage, Help Wanted*' . . . That's . . . where we're going to be getting massages from — there!"

Conversation soon turned to Dolic's fate.

"What started him [toward arrest was that] instead of selling his fucking weed," DaSilva said, "he started exchanging his product [for cocaine] . . . This is what hurt him . . . [U.S. authorities] don't come and bring you down south for fucking weed. That [cocaine] product's a killer, man. That's the one they fucking go after."

Day said, "Well, listen, um, also, uh — what's his name [Bob DeRosa] said he's bringing in 200 [kilos of cocaine]."

"I don't care," DaSilva said. "Not interested . . . it's the worst possible. Listen, that's the plague, man . . . It's the black fucking plague, that's what it is."

"What's it worth now?"

"Who cares?"

"Well, [Bob DeRosa] asked me."

"[Cocaine] is going to start to be worth a lot of money right now, because you heard about . . . [Agostino] Cuntrera, who got killed last week in Montreal . . . Cuntrera is the same family you guys got in Toronto, but the leading part of the family is in Montreal and Rizzuto's son got killed. The other Rizzuto's in jail, the old man is in hiding, six or seven members of the family have died over the past year. Paolo Rendo went missing somewhere here in Toronto after a meeting and these were the main importers right now, after the bikers, right. Bikers . . . still control part of the ports and all that, but they're not the ones who the Colombians are going to send 1,000 keys [kilograms of cocaine] and 500 keys and, 'You pay me in a month,' you know what I mean. So prices went up now for sure, but irregardless, I'm not interested."

"I'm glad you're not," Day said.

Soon after that, DaSilva wondered if they were being followed by police. Day dropped him off at the Petro Canada on Burlington's Harvester Road, where Guindon and DaSilva's truck were waiting, and DaSilva and Guindon drove to Quebec, followed by police. They stopped only once, for DaSilva to urinate on the side of the highway.

At the border, Sûreté du Québec took over, following the men to their homes, east of Montreal.

. . . . . .

On July 15, Day went to Bob DeRosa's farm, where his large, bearded host complained about his back problems and said he was going to Calgary in a few days. He also mentioned a plan to fly to Cuba, then from there to Panama and then to Colombia. DeRosa asked if Day knew anybody with a container coming into Canada — the container guy he was dealing with wanted 30 percent of the load when it reached Halifax, which was too expensive.

When asked by police-prompted Day about the old Molson grow op and where the profit had gone, DeRosa got aggressive and snarled, "You think I got all of the money?" Indignant, he declared that, for his work at the Molson grow op, he only ever got paid $4,500 every 45 days. Once Oro started, he said, he got $9,000 altogether every 45 days.

Later in their meeting, Day explained the drawbacks with the rent and the electricity at the Welland location. DeRosa tossed around some ideas to solve the problems. He offered to supply Day with 10 pounds of cannabis. He said he had two suppliers: one sold it to him for $2,200 a pound and the other, "the Chinaman," sold it for $1,800 per pound. He said he could drive to Richmond Hill and get Day a sample.

Day left the farm, and before long he received a text from Bob DeRosa, inviting him back that night. When Day returned, DeRosa took a large green shopping bag out of a kitchen cupboard. Inside it were a pair of clear ziplock bags, each holding a pound of flowers. Day removed the bags and opened them. He took out a sample and put it into a smaller ziplock bag.

DeRosa said he bought this cannabis for $2,150 a pound and sold it for $2,200, for a profit of $50 a pound. Could Day take 10 pounds?

Day said he would take the sample to his contact and get an answer later. (The answer from the OPP would be "Yes, please!")

Day asked about the two Glocks — the price of $4,000 seemed a bit high to him. DeRosa said he was still working on getting them from the Six Nations reserve, then said, "If you can get them cheaper, maybe I should buy them off of you," and reminded Day that the price included two clips for each gun, plus ammunition.

On July 20, at 7:10 a.m., Bob DeRosa got into his wife's blue Jeep and drove to a variety store and a Tim Hortons in Elmvale, then drove home. After a few hours had passed, he left home again, this time driving to the Vaughan Mills shopping mall. He parked in a handicap spot.

At 10:30 a.m., a gray Lexus SUV pulled into the mall lot. A child who looked to be about two years old was inside the SUV. DeRosa got out of his Jeep and met the driver of the Lexus, a bald Asian male in his early 30s. They stood together and had a short conversation, while the child stayed inside the vehicle. The Asian man opened the hatch of the SUV and took out a red-and-white-checkered bag, which he handed to DeRosa, who took it to his Jeep and put it in the back.

Police followed the gray Lexus, which drove to a plaza, where the driver picked up another child. The driver, now with two children in the vehicle, drove to yet another plaza, then to Highgate Public School in Markham, then to the nearby Metro Square Mall, the Finila Midland Centre in Scarborough, Super International Car Rentals, Enrich International Travel Inc. and finally a condominium in Scarborough, where police surveillance of the SUV driver and the clueless kids ended.

Later, DeRosa again texted Day, saying he was home and inviting Day to visit.

When he got there, Day was led into the kitchen, where his host took a box out from behind a chair. Inside were five one-pound bags of cannabis. At $2,200 a pound, DeRosa explained, the box cost $11,000. Day said he had brought only $10,000, as he'd thought the buy was at

$1,800 a pound. DeRosa agreed to accept the outstanding $1,000 later, and Day handed him $10,000 in Ontario taxpayers' money.

DeRosa said he had another cannabis supplier who could sell 50 pounds a week at $1,700 a pound. He also mentioned that he was leaving on Friday for South America, by way of Cuba, to arrange the big cocaine shipment.

Two days later, Day and DeRosa met at a 7-Eleven gas station, where "The Indian" gave "The Deaf Guy" the $1,000 he owed. DeRosa said he had a sample of the $1,700 cannabis for Day, but had forgotten it at home. Saying it was "good shit, real green and dry," he suggested that Day drop by the farm later and pick up the sample.

As for the Glocks, DeRosa said they were coming from the U.S. and would definitely arrive soon. He would let Day know when they did.

The next time Day and the OPP heard from Bob DeRosa, it was via a text sent from somewhere in South America.

When are you coming back to Canada, Day texted.

In a week, DeRosa texted back, asking if everything was okay.

Everything is good, Day texted. He added that there was someone in Canada he wanted DeRosa to meet.

Ok, Bob DeRosa replied.

. . . .

Jeff DaSilva was in Walton — a village in Huron County, near Goderich, Ontario — with his two sons for a big motocross competition. His talented boys had won multiple Canadian motocross championships while getting straight As at school.

Day came to the competition to meet DaSilva, who introduced him to his runner, Yvan Guindon, who had a silver-colored, three-quarter-ton pickup. DaSilva said he was sitting on 200 pounds of outdoor cannabis ready for distribution and could, on an ongoing basis, sell Day 100 pounds of indoor a week. For cash deals, DaSilva said, he could meet "anywhere, anytime, for any amount."

They discussed a code for texts — they would refer to outdoor cannabis as "landscape work" and indoor cannabis as "construction work."

DaSilva said he did not like the Welland location. It was too far, too old, needed too much upkeep and did not have the right electrical supply. He told Day to have DeRosa find them a site in Oshawa or Kingston — anywhere east of Toronto, to be more convenient for DaSilva and his Quebec-based crew. If the lease payments were $7,000 a month, he said, they would need at least 100 candles to make it profitable.

When Day next met DeRosa, at the Husky at highways 400 and 88, Constable Sanders was there too, again posing as an underworld figure. After introducing DeRosa to Sanders, Day told him that DaSilva did not like the Welland location and wanted something east of the GTA. DeRosa said he would start looking right away.

After Sanders left, DeRosa told Day he had 50 kilos of his own cocaine sitting in Panama — in terms of quality, "the best of the best." He said that the way smuggling deals with the Colombians worked was that the Colombians would match every load one for one, making this load to Canada 100 kilos — half belonging to the Colombians, half to Bob DeRosa. Twenty-one percent of the total load would go to the "door" (the person who got the drugs out of the shipping container when it arrived at a Canadian port). DeRosa complained about the commission charged by his door and wanted to know if Day knew anybody who could get the drugs out of the container more cheaply. Day suggested Sanders.

Bob DeRosa had lots of big plans for his partnership with the undercover officer. He talked about working with "the Chinese" to smuggle the illegal dust into Canada inside seafood — giving examples of tilapia, snapper, tuna, popo, squid and octopus — or arranging something with a particular well-known international coffee company, to hide cocaine in its shipments. When the cocaine scheme really started rolling, DeRosa predicted, he would go live in South America to take care of business there, while Day handled things in Canada.

He said he wanted to talk again with Day's contact, Sanders, and Day arranged it. The lunchtime meeting was set for Barrie, at a Tim Hortons on Essa Road. Day was not invited. On the drive north, Sanders listened nonstop to Toronto radio station The Edge; about half an hour of 102.1 FM's music and DJ banter was recorded on the OPP machine under his clothes, including the songs "Bulls on Parade" by Rage Against the Machine, "Midlife Crisis" by Faith No More and Radiohead's "Paranoid Android."

Sanders and Bob DeRosa met in the doughnut store and sat down to talk. They discussed Glocks, grow ops and large-scale cocaine smuggling while customers came in and left with bagels and Boston creams. DeRosa said he was working with two cartels in Colombia. He knew an Italian guy who had been recently set free after 17 years in a Mexican jail and died three months later. His widow was Colombian and their son, DeRosa claimed, was his contact to the Santa Marta cartel. The cartel also had someone going to school in Calgary whom he dealt with.

DeRosa said the Colombians wanted a 10 percent deposit up front. There were 50 kilos right now in Panama — 25 his, 25 belonging to the Colombians. (Telling the story to Day a few days earlier, DeRosa had said there were 100 kilos in Panama, 50 his and 50 the Colombians'.) For 25 kilos, DeRosa explained, the deposit would be $100,000. He said he could sell a piece of equipment and get $40,000 to contribute. Sanders said he might be able to come up with the remaining $60,000.

Bob DeRosa explained that there were two ways to smuggle in the cocaine: "One, the Colombians transport it here on a container; we just need a door across the border for them. Two, we use our own container and bring it in ourselves."

Sanders thought option two was best and said he could arrange a container. DeRosa said that when the load was ready, Sanders could meet him in Cuba, but Sanders disagreed, saying Panama would be better. Then DeRosa offered to take Sanders to Colombia, to introduce the undercover OPP officer to members of the Santa Marta cocaine cartel.

Bob DeRosa also spoke of wanting to move to Colombia to open a café.

Briefing

From the report of the Canadian Government Commission of Inquiry into the Non-Medicinal Use of Drugs, 1972:

"The short-term physical effects of cannabis (apart from those which affect psychomotor abilities) are relatively insignificant on normal persons, and there is as yet no evidence of serious long-term physical effects."

"There has been little evidence in Canada to support an association of cannabis with crimes of violence. Nor is there any suggestion that cannabis users are obliged to engage to any significant extent in a career of petty crime to support their habit."

"Many users of cannabis exhibit high ethical standards, apart from their wilful violation of the drug laws."

"[T]he extraordinary methods of law enforcement which must be resorted to because of the difficulty in detecting offences by reason of the fact that there is seldom, if ever, a complainant. The use of special methods of search, undercover agents and informers, and police encouragement of offences makes the impact of the criminal law process in this field particularly unpleasant and generates considerable resentment."

"The costs to a significant number of individuals, the majority of whom are young people, and to society generally, of a policy of prohibition of simple possession are not justified by the potential for harm of cannabis . . . We, therefore, recommend the repeal of the prohibition against the simple possession of cannabis. The cultivation of cannabis should be subject to the same penalties as trafficking, but it should not be a punishable offence unless it is cultivation for the purpose of trafficking."

. . . .

From the report of the Canadian Senate Special Committee on Illegal Drugs, 2002:

"Cannabis presents almost no toxicity and cannot lead to an overdose . . . psychological dependency is relatively minor. In fact, it cannot be compared in any way with tobacco or alcohol dependency . . . physical dependency on cannabis is virtually non-existent."

"Most long-term users integrate their use into their family, social and occupational activities; and cannabis itself is not a cause of other drug use. In this sense, we reject the gateway theory . . . Cannabis itself is not a cause of delinquency and crime; and cannabis is not a cause of violence."

"Due to the consensual nature of drug offences, police have been granted substantial enforcement powers and have adopted highly intrusive investigative techniques . . . Over 90,000 drug-related incidents are reported annually by police; more than three-quarters of these incidents relate to cannabis . . . The uneven application of the law is of great concern and may lead to discriminatory enforcement, alienation of certain groups within society, and creation of an atmosphere of disrespect for the law; in general, it raises the issue of fairness and justice."

"Police and court costs . . . to enforce the cannabis laws [not including the costs of jails and prisons] . . . may be estimated to represent a total of $300 to $500 million per annum."

"Every year, over 20,000 Canadians are arrested for cannabis possession. This figure might be as high as 50,000 . . . However, even those numbers are laughable when compared to the three million people who have used cannabis over the past 12 months."

"As far as cannabis is concerned, only behaviour causing demonstrable harm to others should be prohibited: illegal trafficking, selling to minors and impaired driving."

"[U]sed in moderation, cannabis in itself poses very little danger to users and to society as a whole . . . In addition to being ineffective and costly, criminalization leads to a series of harmful consequences: users are marginalized and exposed to discrimination by the police and the criminal justice system; society sees the power and wealth of organized crime enhanced as criminals benefit from prohibition . . . We have demonstrated that criminal law is not an appropriate governance tool for matters relating to personal choice and that prohibition is known to result in harm which often outweighs the desired positive effects."

"The Committee recommends that the Government of Canada declare an amnesty for any person convicted of possession of cannabis under current or past legislation."

# The Trap Closes

"I told Bob, you can't trust anyone!"
— Glenn Day

DaSilva texted Day on September 7, 2010: *Hello, he's there what your [estimated time of arrival?].* When Day got the text, he went to meet DaSilva's runner, Yvan Guindon, at the Husky near the Molson plant.

Day recognized the gray-haired Guindon, in blue jeans and a T-shirt, from the motocross races in Walton. He parked beside Guindon's blue Chevrolet Cobalt sports car. There was little conversation between English-speaking Day and French-speaking Guindon. Guindon took 20 pounds of cannabis in garbage bags from the backseat of his car and put it in the trunk of Day's car. As he was carrying the cannabis from one vehicle to the other, one bag of it fell to the pavement and Guindon bent over to pick it up.

Day gave Guindon $25,000, and the runner left, driving north on 400 to the Wasaga Beach area, where he pulled up at Robert Bleich's home. Guindon opened the trunk of his Cobalt and took out two black garbage bags, one black duffel bag and three ziplock bags, all full of cannabis, and put them into the box of Bleich's Toyota Tundra.

After the five-minute transaction, DaSilva's runner drove, making a call on his cell phone, to Highway 401 eastbound. He stopped at the Fifth Wheel Truck Stop in Bowmanville, then headed straight back to Quebec. At the border, the OPP surveillance team was again replaced by Sûreté du Québec.

Meanwhile, Bleich, after getting the cannabis from Guindon, took it to his unit at the nearby Clearview Self Storage, then drove to a Royal Bank near his home. Later, he went to a Foodland grocery store, then home.

Soon afterwards, Day received a text from DaSilva, who had gotten a text from Bleich saying he thought he was being observed by police. DaSilva forwarded to Day the last text he had received from Bleich: *Bro there is heat everywhere since u left.*

The next day, Bleich phoned Day, saying he "ha[d] heat." Bleich sounded nervous and agitated. He was sure the police were onto him and following him. About his cell phone, Bleich said, "I tossed it. It's bugged."

Bleich later recalled, "I noticed I was being followed for three months after the last meeting with Glenn Day. It was so noticeable it was crazy. There'd always be three to four cars, always the same cars. The organized crime unit was following me. Out of Orillia . . . I was being tailed. Lost the cops once. On the way to Haliburton there are a couple of windy roads. [The unmarked police cars] were back one kilometer. I did a quick right and up a hill. The cop cars went by. I went back the other way to my uncle's, where I pulled in and sat and watched them going back and forth for an hour, looking for me."

Day started buying cannabis directly from DaSilva, without Bleich's involvement. His next order from DaSilva was for 10 pounds of indoor, at $1,750 a pound, and 30 pounds of outdoor, at $1,250 a pound.

Day and DaSilva made arrangements to meet near Montreal soon.

. . . .

On September 16, 2010, Day went to DeRosa's bison farm to talk about a potential grow-op location in an abandoned shoe factory near Kingston. Day saw two people sitting on the front porch — DeRosa's wife and a man in his 60s, with short brown-and-gray hair, wearing a hat and coat. He was saying something to Mrs. DeRosa about how the weather here was cool compared to Cuba.

Bob DeRosa came out and, without introducing Day to the man, guided him down the driveway to a spot near three parked cars: a black Pontiac Sunfire, an older model green Impala and Bob DeRosa's wife's blue Jeep Cherokee.

Glenn Day lifted a hand and made his fingers look like a gun, wordlessly asking about the two Glocks. "Be patient," said DeRosa. There was a delay because his contact for the guns had gotten into an argument with his wife and been arrested on domestic violence charges.

As for the cocaine shipment, DeRosa said, "I'm this close." He had just "sent down" another $3,000 to show the Colombians he was still serious about the 50 kilos sitting in Panama. DeRosa was also eager to meet with Sanders again, so Day took out his cell phone and arranged a meeting between the two men at a Tim Hortons in Vaughan, at Highway 400 and Major Mackenzie Drive.

When the smuggler and the undercover officer met at the doughnut store the next day, DeRosa was with two people: an older man, described as his interpreter for dealing with the Colombians, and a 30-year-old blond woman, described as Honduran and also an interpreter. DeRosa said he had 50 kilos of cocaine in Panama now. Sanders wanted to increase the load to 100 kilos. DeRosa agreed, adding that the price in Panama was $4,000 to $5,000 a kilo. The door would be 22 percent. DeRosa said that, for a load of this size, they would need to pay the cartel $200,000 up front and that he could kick in $60,000. Constable Sanders said he could come up with the remaining $140,000.

Sanders suggested DeRosa invite the Colombians to visit Canada for a meeting, and DeRosa agreed, saying he would send the cartel members money for their plane tickets.

. . . . . .

The next week, Glenn Day and Constable Jones drove to the Montreal area in a pickup truck. On the way, DaSilva texted them directions to the meeting location, a steakhouse in a commercial strip mall near Highway 30. DaSilva arrived in a white van and told Day and Jones to park in a nearby underground garage.

When DaSilva asked Day if he had the "buy money," Day gave him $5,000 in a bundle. Jones was asked to leave the area for an hour, and DaSilva and Day went into the steakhouse. Day mentioned that Guindon had dropped some of the cannabis on the pavement during the last transaction. DaSilva complained that Bleich owed him $15,000 for a previous order and asked Day for Bleich's phone number. Day said Bleich had thrown the phone away, thinking it was bugged.

DaSilva said he had brought 30 pounds of outdoor and 10 pounds of indoor for a total price of $55,000. Day said he had brought only $35,000 and maybe he could buy just the indoor, but DaSilva had been counting on getting all of the money, as he had a supplier to pay. DaSilva used the calculator in his phone to work out ways to deal with the cash shortfall. Day mentioned DeRosa's efforts to get a location near Kingston, but DaSilva did not seem interested; he just stared at his calculator and entered numbers.

After the meeting, they met the undercover police officer outside. DaSilva and Day got into DaSilva's van and Jones was told to wait in a nearby strip club. Day noticed six or seven big cardboard boxes in the van's cargo area. DaSilva said each box contained eight pounds of outdoor cannabis and that he could not return it.

They drove to another commercial parking lot, where DaSilva took Day's truck. He said he had to fill the order at his house, which was a two-minute drive away. When DaSilva returned, he told Day he had "fronted" some of their order and Day owed him $11,400. He said he had put into the box of Day's pickup a cardboard box containing eight pounds of outdoor cannabis and a drum with 20 pounds of outdoor and 400 grams of indoor.

As Day and Jones were driving west toward Ontario, Day got a text from DaSilva, who communicated that he sensed "heat." He asked Day to return the extra eight pounds he had fronted him, as he was in no position to lose any profits. DaSilva sent a further series of worried texts to Day, describing the potential police vehicles following Day:

I'm sure you're not alone right now, watch out for a black SUV.

Watch for the black SUV, has a plate in the front of it.

Call me when you pass where we had lunch together [Kingston].

Eventually, DaSilva seemed to calm down. The next day, Day got a text from him: *Everything OK.*

The day after that, Bob DeRosa and Constable Sanders met again at the same Husky Truck Stop. Sanders said the container for the cocaine was ready to go; he just had to make a phone call. "There's a refrigerated container," he said. "It's done, perfect. It's good to go for sure."

Bob DeRosa said "the Colombian" (his contact in the Santa Marta cartel) was in Europe, maybe Amsterdam, and that he was trying to get him to come to Toronto to meet Sanders. "This is just between you and me and nobody else," he told Sanders, and described for the undercover officer a convoluted plan to make a higher-than-normal profit in the cocaine smuggling scheme. Instead of paying somebody 20 to 22 percent to be the door, DeRosa explained, "we are the door [making use of Sanders' supposed contact at Halifax harbour] . . . We take the 30 percent for the door. That leaves us 70 kilos — 35 are the Colombians' and 35 are ours. We sell the Colombians' 35 kilos, take a percentage and then give them their money. We then sell our 35 kilos and keep all profits. The Colombians' money is given to them in Canada, either Montreal or Toronto."

From the profit from their 30 percent door fee, DeRosa said, he and Sanders would keep a "slush fund . . . Understand what a slush fund is?"

"We'll put that toward the next one," Sanders said.

"Yeah, that's our fund," DeRosa said. "It pays legals. Pays for, like, a catastrophe, whatever." He talked about using the slush fund to buy future cocaine loads, then ranted to Sanders: "It's getting fucking hard dealing with people you trust. You know, plus there's expenses, you see. I don't use a phone anymore. I get on a plane, I go. The last time I was gone six weeks. It costs money, you know, that. I go here, I go there, I go there. How long do you want to go with this thing? You want to go by guts?"

"Yeah," Sanders said. "What I'm saying is, if something doesn't seem right, we will just keep it quiet for a little while."

"For sure," DeRosa said. "I usually put some — I say, 'Listen, let's go, let's do, all right, that's great.' You know what I'm saying? If something is not smooth, we stop . . . I've never had a problem. I've never had a problem. I've known him [the cartel contact] since '75. I will be honest with you, I've known him since '75 in Panama, you know what I mean?"

The cocaine he now had stored in Panama was the very best quality, DeRosa said: "AAA stuff. Not A, not AA. Triple A." He told Sanders they were partners and had to trust each other.

Soon after that, Day texted DaSilva, saying he would be sending his runner, Jones, to make a payment on the money owed for the cannabis picked up near Montreal.

DaSilva texted back, asking, *Can he be trusted, will payment be in full.*

Day texted that Jones could be trusted and *No will only be partial payment.*

DaSilva texted, *Has the kid [Jones] met my runner?*

No, Day texted.

DaSilva texted, *Sending my runner [Guindon], meet 12 noon Home Depot* [in Cornwall on October 4].

Yvan Guindon arrived at the Home Depot in a blue GM pickup, wearing blue jeans and a black hoodie. Jones arrived later, walked to Guindon's truck and got inside. Guindon said his name was "Yvan the Terrible." The transaction took less than a minute. Guindon took $3,000 from the undercover officer, then drove back east to Oka.

. . . . . .

When Bob DeRosa and Sanders met, he reminded Sanders of his agreement to contribute the remainder of the money for the deposit, as well as a container to bring the cocaine to Halifax. "Do you have the container numbers?" he asked.

"I can get it," Sanders said.

Regarding the deposit money, Sanders said he had $200,000 coming in the next night. He kept trying to convince DeRosa to delay his flight, supposedly so that Sanders could fly down with him.

DeRosa repeatedly said no to the delay — his cartel contact had already flown to Cuba and was waiting. "They called and said it was an emergency and that's why I fucking booked right away. As soon as they called me, I called you . . . [The cartel members are] good people. So we want to work together. They are really good, they get premium dollar, their word is gold. I do a lot of business with them, their word is gold. I tell you, I've known them for years and years and years." He showed Sanders a recent text on his phone, explaining that it was from a cartel member. The undercover officer made a mental note of the sender's Spanish-sounding name.

Apparently open to changing their previous plans about the door to Canada, DeRosa said he knew a "Chinese guy" who worked as a door at the airport, charging 30 percent. He said that drugs were smuggled differently on different airlines: on CanJet, contraband was hidden in the belly of the plane, while on Air Canada and Caribbean Airlines, it was concealed in the baggage.

DeRosa again invited Sanders to meet the Colombian cartel members in Havana: "I'll come and get you at either airport."

"Okay."

"You understand."

"Yup."

"Don't take a cab, nothing. Just wait there. I'm there."

"Okay."

"If I'm a few minutes late, just be patient."

"Okay."

. . . .

From the handwritten report of Glenn Day, October 6, 2010:

> *Meet with [Officers] Rick, Rob and Sergeant Paul for lunch in Barrie.*
>
> *I was told to text Bob [DeRosa].*
>
> *I texted Bob, Hey Bob, hoping we can hook up tomorrow at your place. I need 5 of what I got from you before. Let me know if you can do it?*
>
> *Bob texted back, I can, but out of town . . . I will be back friday sometime.*
>
> *I was told to text back, Not a big rush, this can be done the early part of next week. I'll text you monday or tuesday to let you know.*
>
> *I asked if he was coming back with a tan [from being in the south]?*
>
> *Bob texted back, I will call you tomorrow when I be back.*
>
> *I text back, OK, I'll wait for your call.*
>
> *Bob texted, OK cool!*

From the handwritten report of Glenn Day, October 11, 2010:

> *Receive a text from Bob, Are you back yet? I'm at home if you want to drop by . . .*
>
> *I text back, Still driving, long weekend. Hope to be there just after 8:30 pm.*
>
> *Bob texted, OK.*
>
> *. . . [Officer] Rick went over my objectives . . . and gave me one more that was I was to order 10 lbs of weed from Bob and not the five I asked for before.*

I arrived at Bob's house at 8:30 pm.

I rang the doorbell and Bob answered. He invited me in. I sat at the table, he offered me something to drink and I told him water.

There were two jeeps in the driveway.

The guy with the straw hat was on the other side of the room, smoking.

Bob told me that he had talked to Mark [Sanders] today.

He asked if Mark was looking after me. I told him that we had worked it out.

I asked him where he [had been] and he told me that he [had been] in the U.S.

I asked when he was leaving. He told me his wife was driving him to the airport at 3:00 am . . . that he was only going for a week 7/8 days, that he had a doctor's appointment and could not miss it.

His friend in the straw hat was going with him. He was his interpreter. He spoke Spanish.

They were each bringing $10,000 in cash.

He said he was hoping to meet with Mark down there on Thursday and wanted Mark to bring $10,000 as well.

He told me to always check my phone . . .

Bob said all is ready to go, he said Mark told him he had $200,000.

Mark was putting in $160,000 and Bob had $60,000.

There [were] 50 keys ready.

He said Mark wanted more but settled on the 50.

. . . I told Bob that I needed the 10 lbs for this time tomorrow night and if I wasn't there to pick it up, I would be there on Wed morning before 9:00 am.

I asked the price. He said it's the same, 2,150 + 50 for him . . .

He said it was really good this time . . .

Bob [said that] if there is anyone you can trust, it's Glenn, that we go back a long way, to the Molson plant and the Oro center. I told Bob, you can't trust anyone!

I asked Bob if he was able to get rid of the coke once it was here and he said it would all be gone to the Chinese . . .

I left Bob's house and . . . met [Officers] Rick and Rob, back in Barrie at the staging point, at which time I was debriefed. Rick and Ross left and I started my notes.

I finished up just after 12:30 am, then went to bed.

. . . .

The next morning, frustrated OPP officers at Pearson International Airport watched Bob DeRosa and another man board a Sunwing Airlines flight to Holguín, Cuba. They wanted to arrest him, but the timing was wrong. The plan was to arrest all the suspects at the same time, on a predetermined schedule. Moving too soon could put Day, Sanders and Jones in danger.

Bob DeRosa flew south.

Later that day, in Barrie, an Ontario judge signed a search warrant for the farmhouse and land where DeRosa lived with his family.

. . . .

Wednesday, October 13, 2010. Phelpston.

At around 10 a.m, OPP officers assigned to Project Birmingham showed up at Bob DeRosa's bison farm. They found some dismantled grow-op equipment in a tractor trailer. When the officers told DeRosa's wife about the search warrant, she said, "I know what you are looking for," and took them to a nylon bag in their kitchen. In the bag was 10 pounds of dried cannabis flowers. In a separate building on the farm, they found a grow op that was no longer in use.

Elsewhere that morning, OPP officers — with the assistance of officers from Sûreté du Québec and Niagara Regional Police — simultaneously arrested Davorka Pelikan, Yvan Guindon, Robert Bleich, Jeff DaSilva, Denis Hould, Larry McGee and Fred Freeman.

Also arrested was Pierre Homard — the same man who had, years ago, bought the grow op in Kawartha Lakes that Bleich, Day and Scott Walker had built. More recently, Homard had hired Day to work on his house and Day had collected evidence against him. Police wiretaps for Project Birmingham had caught this man talking with Day about smuggling 1,000 kilos of cannabis oil from India to Canada. (Later, all charges against Homard would be dropped.)

At the time of his arrest, Fred "Goggles" Freeman had left the car-wash industry and was a chicken farmer, having spent nine months experimenting in his barn with special "nutrient dense" chicken and eggs. His wife worked at a Niagara-area greenhouse, helping to raise poinsettias, mums and other legal flowers. Freeman and his wife had four daughters.

Bleich was the only person to be charged in both the 2004 and 2010 police sweeps. At the time of this second arrest, his landscaping/construction/tree-cutting company, All of the Above, was doing well. This company — which had previously renovated a customer loading area at an IKEA store in Burlington and billed $47,000 for five weeks' work and a job well done — had been about to sign another contract with the Burlington IKEA.

Bleich later described his arrest: "I was at home. I had a house in the country. A four-bedroom house; an older house, 35 years old, brick, with 38 acres that someone else farms, hay and corn . . . It was 10 a.m., I'd just finished a bowl of Cheerios and 2% milk. Just went to put the bowl in the kitchen sink, rinse it. I was about to put it in the dishwasher. Out the window, I see 15 cops in black on foot and their cars on the street. They were running at the house from different angles. I knew I was fucked. I had $5,000 in my pocket I tossed in the garbage can under the sink for my wife, but they found it. Bang on the door, 'Let us in!' They knew I had dogs, they had a dog guy at the door wearing a bite suit . . . [He carried] a pry bar, about to use it. I opened the wood door and said, 'You guys ever heard of knocking?' . . . I had two dogs, boxers. Both were loose. I stuck one in its cage. The other, I was holding [by the collar]. I said to the police, 'I've got a dog. Let me put it in the crate.' 'No, open the door.' I flicked the latch on the screen door. The dog guy was in first. They came in and followed me to the dog cage where I put the other dog in. Cuffs, read me the charges and my rights. Later on, I realized it was all because of Glenn Day. They searched me and sat me at the kitchen table and let me phone my lawyer [Randall Barrs]. A cop phoned my wife at work, left a message. The house was messed up by the search. They tore out cupboards. They found the $5,000 in the garbage, $3,200 in a drawer. There were no drugs in the house. Never any drugs in the house. Drove me to Newmarket. Fingerprints. After a few hours, they drove me to Alliston. Interrogation — showing me all these pictures of people and grow ops. Then I heard Glenn Day's voice, recorded when we were playing golf. The cop I had dinner with [Sanders] opens the door: 'Don't you remember me, Mr. Bleich?' 'No.' Back to Newmarket police station . . . I saw everybody coming in: Dove, Freeman, one by one. Then to Lindsay Correctional, waiting for bail."

Soon after this arrest, Bleich would be diagnosed with a blood clot in his leg, prescribed Warfarin blood thinners and given a special sock to wear.

Police announced charges against Drago Dolic of Pollock, Louisiana, and Robert DeRosa of Phelpston, Ontario, both of whom were out of Canada at the time.

The commander of the OPP's Organized Crime Enforcement Bureau sent out a press release announcing the charges and arrests, adding, "We know the vast majority of marihuana grown in Ontario is for export to the U.S. and returns to Canada as cocaine, cash or guns, to support criminal enterprises. Project Birmingham is a great example of a multi-jurisdictional investigation that demonstrates dedication and teamwork required to keep Ontario communities safe."

OPP Constable Peter Leon told a Barrie radio station that the people charged were the "operating minds" of the massive Molson grow op. Another officer told journalists the gang "had no name" and did business apart from biker gangs and traditional organized crime groups.

Detective Inspector Andy Karski of the OPP's criminal investigations branch, the lead investigator for Project Birmingham, said, "This group isn't like a biker gang where there's a hierarchy. Crime is basically their full-time job and they come to the table out of opportunity." Karski added, "It was a complex investigation. It takes a lot of time to infiltrate the group, which is based on trust and relationships." He said the accused people "blended into the community. Neighbours were unaware crime was right on their doorstep . . . Some of these people's neighbours are police officers." He said the cannabis involved was sold in the local market. "I'm confident we've put a dent into the product available out there."

Using the "proceeds of crime" law, the OPP's Provincial Asset Forfeiture Unit seized the old Molson property in Barrie, as well as cash, three vehicles (two pickups and an SUV) and Hould's Elliot Lake house, valued at $55,000.

Constable Leon was photographed standing with a black-and-white police car by the property where the brewery had once stood. A large banner was fastened to the fence, announcing: THIS PROPERTY HAS BEEN RESTRAINED BY POLICE AS OFFENCE-RELATED PROPERTY.

Karski, asked about the seizure of the Barrie land, claimed that Bob DeRosa was an active director in Fercan, the corporation that owned the land. "He has a controlling interest in the company," Karski said.

The land was for sale, with an asking price of $10.7 million. A Barrie real estate agent was looking for a buyer, despite the lien on the property. She said there had been some interest shown by potential buyers. The focus of the forfeiture was the money, not the land itself. "As I understand it," she said, "I'm still able to go ahead and sell the property," with proceeds going into a government-controlled escrow account.

Bob DeRosa was scheduled to return to Canada on October 20. Police were waiting for him at Pearson International Airport, but he never arrived — a Sunwing Airlines representative said he was not on the flight's passenger list. A Canada-wide arrest warrant was issued, eventually followed by the Ottawa offices of the Department of Justice filing an Interpol "Red Notice" (requesting all foreign governments to arrest Bob DeRosa and send him back to Canada).

Toronto defense lawyer Randall Barrs — who had represented all of the gardeners in 2004 — now represented most of the masterminds. In court, Barrs said, "When the arrests happened at Molson [in 2004], it got a ton of publicity in Barrie and all the media was there and there were hundreds of people outside the court cheering these guys on. You're in ski country. You know, it's 'Rocky Mountain High,' whether it's Vancouver or the Laurentians, Northern Ontario, the Rockies — these guys were like local heroes. You know, pot guys, that's all they are."

Barrs spoke harshly of Glenn Day, pointing out his 10-year sentence in Florida for buying Jamaican cannabis oil, his failure to wear a recording device while visiting Dolic in the Louisiana prison and the fact that "the defense does not have Day's agreement [with the OPP] but knows it's a monetary one and he may have been paid hundreds of thousands of dollars, taxpayers' money."

The lawyer also told a journalist that Day had been so incompetent that Dolic had had to fire him for losing rented equipment at Ssonix.

. . . .

Larry McGee's lawyer said, "Anyone in my client's position would find themselves sort of in a tough spot when they're confronted by people like Mr. [Bob] DeRosa, people like the police agent who was used in this matter. These are intimidating and dangerous people and I think anybody who was involved with them in any way would want to be very careful about what they said, and I think [the prosecutor] knows from the disclosure in this case that at one point in time — I'm not sure if it was Mr. [Bob] DeRosa or who made these comments — but there was a belief that my client was in fact the informant; that he had somehow let the police find out about the operation at the Molson plant and there was some talk about killing him at one point in time. Or some suggestion was made to that effect.

"That's not something that my client wasn't aware of before we viewed the disclosure. He was aware through the community. There were hundreds of people who knew about the Molson plant operation. There were all kinds of rumors and talk flying around for the seven years between the time the operation was dismantled and the discussion with the police agent. So my client knew how he was perceived by some of the other people involved, so when he's approached by them again, if you can well imagine, he's on thin ice and has to be careful about what he says and he . . . certainly found himself in a difficult position."

Briefing

Serving 4 million or so passengers a year, staff at Cuba's José Martí airport makes an effort to detect the smuggling of illegal drugs with X-ray machines, long-range scanning video cameras, biometric readers, sniffer dogs and an ion spectrometer.

Despite that, José Martí airport is often used by smugglers (also known as "mules") with plastic-wrapped lumps of dry white powder hidden in their intestines, arriving from Colombia and changing flights in Cuba en route to Europe. Most of the cocaine passing through Cuba goes to Russia (the cocaine markets in Moscow and St. Petersburg began just after the 1917 Bolshevik Revolution) or Holland.

Cuban law includes the death penalty for smuggling drugs, and Cuban judges order it, even in cases when the culprits are top military officers.

Cuban dictator Fidel Castro made bloodthirsty speeches, demanding that more drug smugglers be killed. Those who were caught and not killed usually served long terms in bad prisons.

Governments in Cuba, China and the former Soviet Union are the harshest and cruelest in the world to people caught with illegal drugs.

The Leopard

"This is the first time the [Ontario Provincial Police] has ever gone to Cuba." — OPP Detective Inspector Andy Karski

The RCMP's liaison officer in Cuba let local police know that Bob DeRosa was wanted for drug and weapons offences in Canada and was now probably in Cuba. In November, the liaison officer contacted the officers running Project Birmingham, telling them that DeRosa had been found in Cuba and was now under surveillance.

Bob DeRosa talked to his mother on the phone about once a week. He told her he was in Cuba to get medical treatments for his back and that the warm weather was doing him good. He'd be returning to Canada for further medical treatments, he said. During one such phone call, DeRosa mentioned the Project Birmingham arrests, saying, "Ma, don't worry about what you hear, because what they have put in the papers, I never did all of those things — that's it."

He often told her affectionately, "Mother, I'll see you soon."

On Saturday, December 13, 2010, DeRosa went to Terminal 3 of José Martí International Airport, a concrete structure about 30 miles outside of Havana. He went to the newly refurbished upper level, walking past an information desk and some bars and restaurants open 24 hours a day, and prepared to board a flight to Ecuador — unlike

238

Cuba, Ecuador had no extradition treaty with Canada.

But before he could board the plane, he was arrested by Cuban authorities and caged. He had a choice between staying in jail in Cuba to fight extradition in the Cuban courts or waiving that right and agreeing to return to Canada. In a Cuban courtroom, DeRosa chose the latter and was put onto a commercial flight back home, escorted by OPP Detective Inspector Andy Karski.

Karski later told journalists that DeRosa's "role is obviously significant. This is the first time the OPP has ever gone to Cuba." He added, "The Cuban authorities were very cooperative and very eager to assist the OPP's investigation."

When asked about Drago Dolic — facing charges in Canada while serving a 27-year sentence in the U.S. — Karski said, "We're working with the Public Prosecution Service of Canada to determine the next steps in Mr. Dolic's prosecution. The decision has to be made in consultation with all the stakeholders."

At Bob DeRosa's bail hearing in Newmarket, the prosecutor quoted from secretly recorded conversations DeRosa had had with Day: "It's a lot of time if you get caught. I don't want to do a day of time. I can work anywhere in the fucking world" and "I do this drug trafficking . . . because I've got a family to feed." Bail was denied.

DeRosa's lawyer, James Clark, asked permission for his client to return to court the next week by way of a video appearance, not in person: "With his bad back, being in a chain gang and being driven in a van [to and from court] causes him a great deal of pain . . . [As a result of his partial deafness] when he is in court I cannot communicate with him effectively. Him being here in person serves no purpose."

After the court hearing, Clark told a journalist, "He's very disappointed. He misses his family very much and looks forward to putting this behind him."

. . . .

Newmarket. April 14, 2011.

Before being sentenced, Jeff DaSilva was asked if he wished to say anything to the judge. "I'd like to take the time to apologize to the court and to society for what I've done," he said. "I understand what I've done has been wrong and I will, in the future, use my construction and contracting skills for better use — not to harm me or my family in the future."

DaSilva got five years.

Robert Bleich got two and a half years, plus a $16,665 fine.

Before being sentenced, Denis Hould was asked if he wished to say anything to the judge. "Not really," he replied. "I was going to say something, but everything seems to be okay." He got three years and was ordered to pay $24,000, the value of his half of his house, which he had admitted had been bought with money from the Molson grow op.

Davorka Pelikan was sentenced to a year of house arrest, followed by a year's curfew. Dove's sentence was relatively mild because she had health problems. Her lawyer, Barrs, said, "She, although only 47, has a lot of serious medical problems. She did suffer two strokes and she has a lot of damage to her internal organs. She's having her gallbladder removed tomorrow. Her knee is going to be the next thing that has to be operated on. She can barely walk because of the condition of that knee. She has fibromyalgia. She has rheumatoid arthritis and lupus and, due to the two strokes, she has brain damage, especially in terms of her memory."

In court, Pelikan told the judge, "I kind of get confused."

She would spend much of her time under house arrest babysitting her young and severely disabled granddaughter, who lived with one of Pelikan's daughters in the same Mississauga apartment building, one floor down. She was allowed to attend frequent religious services at several churches.

Yvan Guindon — DaSilva's runner from Oka — was handed a $7,500 fine. A longtime employee of Ford Motor Company, as well as a worker at a relative's food farm, Guindon's punishment was lenient because it was his first offence, he was low in the hierarchy and he had not been involved in the Molson grow op.

After these sentencings, Federal Crown Attorney Joseph Selvaratnam told a journalist, "This has been a positive outcome for the investigation, a good outcome for justice. This is part of a larger project."

. . . .

All charges against Fred Freeman were eventually dropped, due to weak evidence against the cannabis farmer turned chicken farmer. "There was no reasonable prospect of conviction," explained Selvaratnam.

. . . .

On April 14, 2011, Bob DeRosa pled guilty to charges of producing cannabis, offering to transfer a prohibited weapon, being part of a criminal organization and conspiracy to import cocaine.

His lawyer entered a letter from a doctor:

> *I have not seen Robert before. He is a self-employed person who attended today with his wife. For several years now, he has suffered from wide spread pain that is quite persistent, is present both at rest and with activity. It is felt both in the upper and lower extremities. He has experienced a significant functional decline and in spite of all this his wife says that he is not depressed and has not suffered a mood or thought disorder. He does have a marked sleep abnormality and is markedly overweight . . . X-rays of the cervical and lumbosacral spine show primarily mild degenerative disease in the neck and moderate to severe degenerative disease in the lower back . . . Based on normal lab work I would surmise that his current symptoms are likely related to chronic pain or Fibromyalgia.*

"Mr. DeRosa," the judge said, "do you wish to say anything before I sentence you?"

"Yes, I would."

"You don't have to say anything, but if you want, now is your chance."

"Yes, I would."

"Go ahead, please."

"Your Honor, I'm very sorry for the trouble I've caused," Bob DeRosa said before the spectators and media in the Newmarket courtroom. "I deeply regret the trouble I've caused my wife in my foolish and illegal deeds. I have to apologize to my brother Vince for my big mouth talking, when he had nothing to do with the grow operations and did not know about them, having trusted me to manage those buildings. I really let him down. I also want to apologize to the court and to the community for my involvement in these crimes. I have to contend with my health problems and plan my future as a law-abiding member of society. Thank you for letting me speak and letting me apologize."

DeRosa was sentenced to seven years in prison, plus a lifetime firearms ban. Federal Crown Selvaratnam called it "a successful outcome." He said DeRosa was a "significant player" in the Molson grow op, but refused to describe him as its kingpin.

. . . .

Detective Inspector Andy Karski told a journalist that the investigation was not over. "Project Birmingham showed that the OPP is relentless in combating organized crime," he said. "Investigations like these never really end and often take us in different directions."

Karski mentioned the Molson property — worth around $10 million and frozen under crime-related property law since October 2010. "The upcoming seizure [or 'forfeiture'] hearings," he said, "will determine who was involved in the illegal marijuana grow operations."

The Stephen Harper federal government — known for its harsh,

Reagan–like approach to cannabis sellers and users — was represented in the forfeiture hearings by Joseph Selvaratnam, supported by a large team of lawyers and staff. In their written application, and in their oral submissions in court, they argued that Vincent DeRosa — the owner of the Fercan corporation that owned the Molson property — was a member of the cannabis-growing conspiracy.

Fercan and DeRosa were represented in the forfeiture process by prominent Toronto criminal defense lawyer Brian Greenspan, who told Margaret Bruineman of the *National Post*, "The government thinks an innocent third party should have their property forfeited. They force us in court for us to prove we're the innocent third party. This is a total reversal of traditional principles. They say, biblically, that Vince DeRosa is his brother's keeper."

The cannabis-related litigation also involved Hamilton-based First Ontario Credit Union (which had a mortgage on the Molson land) and GRVN, a corporation connected to Vincent DeRosa that owned the bison farm in Phelpston where Bob DeRosa had lived with his family and conspired in guns and cannabis, and where the Filipino men had once worked without pay. The federal government asked to take ownership of the bison farm because of Bob DeRosa's crimes. GRVN was represented in Newmarket by William Friedman, a corporate lawyer perhaps best known for his appearance in *The Bodybuilder and I*, a critically acclaimed video documentary (directed by his once-estranged son) about Friedman's performance, at age 59, in a bodybuilding competition.

The case would take a long time, with many preliminary motions and arguments, followed by 37 days (scattered across many months) of witness testimony and oral submissions by lawyers.

On September 11, 2013, in Newmarket courtroom 201, Judge Peter C. West released his decision on the federal forfeiture application. West had been a criminal defense lawyer and part-time prosecutor before the Harper government appointed him a judge in 2008. West was humble and respectful to the public, the media and court staff; away from the bench, he liked cycling, playing his guitar and singing.

West's 80-page decision was sharply critical of the prosecution: "In many instances the Crown misstated the evidence and then relied on that inaccurate evidence to draw inferences." The judge repeatedly criticized the federal team for advancing its case through the "innuendo of suspicion," "impermissible conjecture and speculation" and "improper" questions without foundation.

West concluded, "There is no evidence that Vincent DeRosa knew of the marijuana grow operations at the Molson plant or that he was wilfully blind as to the existence of the marijuana grow operations . . . I accept Vincent DeRosa's evidence that he was completely unaware of his brother's illegal activities until after Robert's arrest . . . Fercan and GRVN, or the directing minds of those two corporations, are innocent."

Just outside the courtroom, Vincent DeRosa, whose corporations would keep the land, was asked how he had felt during the long court battle.

"It was a little challenging," he said.

"How is your brother doing?"

"Bob is doing well."

"How is his health?"

"His health is holding up."

Surrounded by his triumphant legal team, DeRosa walked out of the Newmarket courthouse.

. . . .

Drago Dolic's lawyer in the U.S. successfully appealed Dolic's 324-month sentence.

The U.S. Court of Appeals found that Judge Lynn Hughes had incompetently sentenced Dolic, finding that the Texan judge's many "failures" led to "plain error that affected [Dolic's] substantial rights" and that "these deficiencies were compounded by the egregious fact . . . that [Hughes] never asked Dolic how he was pleading to the charges, guilty or not guilty. Dolic literally never pleaded to anything."

Bleich (right) during his prison sentence [Michael Lea]

Dolic's new sentence — approximately 200 months — means that he may (if he lives that long) get out of U.S. prison as early as 2023, when he'll be 63.

When the U.S. government sends Dolic home, the Canadian government might prosecute him over the Molson grow op — putting Dolic back in another cage, possibly for the rest of his life.

. . . .

While in prison for the second time, Robert Bleich would complete his high school diploma. He did this, he would later say, "to make my daughter proud."

When he was transferred from the harsh Millhaven prison to the minimum-security Frontenac in Kingston, Bleich and another prisoner, Davin Omeir, started a half-acre vegetable garden on the prison grounds. A story about them appeared in the *Kingston Whig-Standard*, with a photo of Bleich and Omeir showing off large containers full of fresh vegetables: beets, zucchini, beans, tomatoes, carrots and a big orange pumpkin. The vegetables went to a local food bank.

In December 2012, about nine years after the Molson building raid, Bleich finished his time in a north-end Hamilton halfway house, where he had to submit frequent urine samples for drug testing. Bleich was let out on full parole.

He moved back north, back to his home and wife and daughter.

He said that cannabis should be legalized: "You never hear of joints killing anyone." But he also warned, "Pot leads to other drugs. It does. You can only get so high, then you want other things to get higher."

Asked about Glenn Day, Bleich said, "It was my fault. My fault for doing what I did. In the beginning, I said some nasty things [about Day]. But it's my own fault. Not his. He chose his path, I chose my path. He's still a rat, though. I'll never be his friend. . . . Punching him in the head is not worth it."

"Do you forgive him?"

"No, I'll never forgive him."

About his future plans, Bleich said, "I have no interest in meeting with the old drug guys. I'm moving on in life, leaving all that shit behind me. Staying out of trouble. I'm doing it for my daughter . . . Do you know how much time I'd get for growing? I'd lose my family. This is my last straw. I'm not going to mess up my daughter for money — she's worth more than that."

After a pause, Bleich added, "But they say a leopard doesn't lose its spots." He laughed. "I hope I lost mine."